Norma
Willingham

# Eating Chocolates AND Dancing IN THE Kitchen

## SKETCHES OF MARRIAGE AND FAMILY

# Tom Plummer

SHADOW MOUNTAIN.

**Library of Congress Cataloging-in-Publication Data**
  Plummer, Tom, 1939–
    Eating chocolates and dancing in the kitchen : sketches of
  marriage and family / Tom Plummer.
      p.      cm.
    ISBN 1-57345-305-6
    1. Marriage–United States.    2. Family–United States.    I Title.
  HQ536.P596      1998
  306.8–dc21                                                    97-32821
                                                                  CIP

Printed in the United States of America

10  9   8   7   6   5   4   3   2   1                          72082

To Louise

Just because she  made dem goo-goo eyes

JUST BECAUSE SHE MADE DEM GOO-GOO EYES
BY JOHN QUEEN AND HUGHIE CANNON

# Contents

## Introduction

# I Didn't Say That! Did I?

*by Louise Plummer*

I'm never sympathetic with my sons when they complain how I write about them. "I didn't say that!" Sam said after I quoted him saying that I looked like a skunk in a black and white dress I'd made for myself.

"You most certainly did," I said.

"You said it yourself."

"I called *myself* a skunk? I don't think so."

"Well, I didn't say it like that—the way you said it."

What he probably meant was that he didn't say it with an

exclamation mark, or he didn't say it with quite the same smarty-pants attitude that I gave him in the essay.

Ed is even more forthcoming. "Don't mind Mom," he tells people. "She's just a liar."

"I'm not a liar," I say. "I write events exactly the way I remember them."

This makes him snort. "Oh please," he says, "you don't remember anything right."

I beg to differ. I do remember the events of my life clearly. If my sons don't remember them exactly the way I do, they are free to write their own versions. I have told them this, knowing that they would rather have facial tics than put pen to paper.

But after reading Tom's essays, in which I appear all too often sounding more bossy, more whiny, more callous, more wacky, and, the worst, more shallow than I care to think about, I have grown more sympathetic with my sons' views. Did I really say that a Miata convertible would fill in the lonely days and weeks while Tom worked in Germany for two months? If I did, I was joking. Does it come across as joking?

Did I really say that it wasn't Tom's body I was

attracted to, but his brains and humor and kindness to old ladies? Surely, at age twenty-one, I also thought his body was pretty important. In fact, I *know* it was. My memory has not dimmed on this point. If his body wasn't/isn't important, then why are we still dancing in the kitchen? I know why and so does he. Will the reader know?

And was I really so callous about all of Tom's entrepreneurial attempts at making extra money? Yes, I was. The truth is, it was much worse than he lets on. He doesn't tell about the time we drove along the North Shore of Lake Superior and found a restaurant for sale with beachfront on the lake and a couple of extra cabins thrown in for good measure. He wanted to open an ice-cream parlor for summer tourists. I followed him around the outside of the restaurant looking into darkened windows at greasy grills and cheesy curtains with little bears on them. "We could do this," he said, his voice optimistic and buoyant.

I'm sure I said something like, "Are you mad? Are you out of your mind? This place is a mess!"

"You could sew new curtains for the windows," he said.

If Tom is suggesting that I sew anything, he's in major denial, and nothing short of whacking him on the side of the head will bring him around.

Which is, perhaps, what I should have done the first time he mentioned ultralights. Tom wanted to fly an ultralight, which is a non-airplane. It is a flying lawn chair, a swing with wings and a lawn-mower motor. If an airplane is a painting, an ultralight is a scribble with a number-five pencil.

Tom, however, spoke about ultralights with a zeal that appealed to my romantic nature: Imagine being able to fly! It only costs six thousand dollars! Less, if you make it yourself! You don't need a pilot's license to fly it! And with the right equipment, you can land on lakes with it!

Ultralights had "yippee skippy" written all over them. So, when he found a company south of St. Paul that let you "test-drive" one, we got in our car with Sam, who was then about two years old, and drove out for an adventure.

Tom paid twenty-five dollars to go up in a two-seater with a trained pilot, but not before he signed papers releasing the flying company of any liability in case of his death, which seemed imminent when I saw the tiny ultralight pushed out of the garage. It was a toy. Two plastic seats with wings attached and a bar to rest your feet on. No cockpit. Tom giggled when he saw it. Still, he strapped himself in next to the pilot, and soon the motor was putt-putting across a field of dried grass, and then they were airborne. Sam and I clapped and cheered and shivered. I tried not to think of double indemnity. The machine rose higher and higher until it was a mosquito against the blue sky. Tom's legs swung loose. "I'm flying!" he yelled down to us.

"Yes, you are!" I called back. Sam clapped. It is a lovely, aching thing to watch someone fulfill even a small dream. The half hour passed quickly. For just another ten dollars, I too, I was told, could go up and dangle in the sky for thirty minutes, but this was not *my* dream, and I declined.

Tom continued to talk about ultralights. I suggested that he build one in the garage, thinking that if he could find a way to get the money, what was the harm?

Then we took another ride up to the North Shore. This time we drove all the way to Grand Marais, where, just outside of town, an old lodge with a sloping lawn was for sale. Tom was ecstatic. "We could run a lodge, buy an ultralight, and fly fishermen to the surrounding lakes. We could have a summer theater, horse and carriage rides, dances. People would come from all over to stay at our lodge—Plummer's Pond (there *was* a pond in back).

I pictured myself making up twenty beds every morning and keeping our sons from biting the guests, but I was calm for one more question: "How would we finance this venture?"

"We'd sell our house and live here year-round."

What did I have to say at such a suggestion, I wonder. Probably something like, "Who's *we*, Mr. *Man?*" Or, "I want a divorce." Or, "Read my lips: No way, José!" I might have said any or all of those or worse. I choose not to remember. In any case, we never made an offer.

I digress. I began by doing what my sons do: complaining. Someone—Tom—who knows me better than anyone, is writing about me, and I'm skittish. So I retaliated by telling a couple of stories about him.

Are Tom's stories true? Are my stories true?

Yes, they are.

No, they aren't.

Both. The events are true in either case. I would have told the stories differently from the way he tells them, and vice versa. I know that he would say he was only kidding about buying that restaurant and turning it into an ice-cream parlor. "I just like to dream," he would say. "She didn't speak to me for the rest of the afternoon just because we got out of the car and looked in the windows of the place." The reason I know what he would say is because we have told that story to friends, correcting each other in the telling.

Perhaps I would feel safer if I could interrupt Tom through these essays the way I do in conversations: "Oh, you weren't just dreaming. Every time you begin looking at something, we end up buying it." Yes. That's what I miss most as I read through these essays. I miss breaking in. I miss saying, "I didn't say that! Did I?"

Ah! Sweet Mys- ter- y of Life, at last I've

found thee, Ah, I know at last the se-cret of it all.

AH! SWEET MYSTERY OF LIFE
BY RIDA JOHNSON YOUNG AND VICTOR HERBERT

# Happy Unbirthday

Louise has told me a zillion times that she never saw a guy more dense than I was about women. I attribute it to a retarded hormonal development. I grew up in an academic fog, spending long hours of study in a room lighted only by high basement windows and being nurtured by parents who were priming me for life as a Mormon Jesuit. And then one night, at a church bowling party, Louise turned on the lights.

Since I had been attending church with the same congregation all my life, I thought I knew pretty well who was interested in me and who was not, and whom I was interested in and whom I was not. Louise was three years younger than I; we had not run in the same circles. Even if I had thought about dating her, which I hadn't, I would have dismissed it, because she was nearly as tall as I—a taboo for my male ego.

Louise, I was to learn, had seen the bowling party in its proper light—a mating ritual in disguise—and was already planning an assault on my dull senses. She was not, she later said, interested merely in my body but in my mind, my piano playing, my kindness to old ladies, and my perverse sense of humor. There's no accounting for taste. Anyway, with not much effort, she managed to join the group on my lane. In my usual introverted mind-set, I was too caught up with applying the principles of my recent bowling class at the university to notice that I was being stalked.

"I'll bet a malt I can beat you," she said in a casual way as I laced my red and green shoes.

"I'll take that bet," I said. If I had considered any number of literary texts or films in that moment, I would have known that competition between sexes, whether by jousting or by wits, is the beginning of the mating game.

The details of the contest have long since faded. To my recollection, we bowled three games. I won all three, albeit by narrow margins.

"You owe me a malt," I said as we parted company.

About ten o'clock that evening, the doorbell rang. I answered to find a malt sitting on the porch. A sign with a hand-drawn bowler read, "To the world's best bowler." A yellow and white 1956 Ford station wagon was disappearing around the corner; I recognized from its taillights and pale color that it belonged to Louise's family.

She later told me that she was driving and had gotten Teddy, her younger brother, to put the malt on the porch, ring the bell, and "run like hell."

The next day I went to Morrow's Nut House in downtown Salt Lake, bought a bag of mixed nuts, and attached a note that read, "Tanks fer da malt. I'm nuts about you too." I sketched a tank (for "tanks") and pasted a picture of Mr. Peanut on the paper. Although Louise has framed the note and even hung it in the house from time to time, I remember it with some embarrassment. How romantic was it to buy a girl a bag of mixed nuts? How charming was it to sketch a tank on a flirtation note and paste a picture of Mr. Peanut alongside it? How classy was it to write the note in pencil?

When I delivered the sack of nuts to Louise, she was sitting on the front porch of her house with a girlfriend. I must have found it doubly awkward. I did, nevertheless, get out of the car and walk over to her. I'm sure the conversation was short.

"Hi."

"Hi."

"I brought you some nuts."

"Gee, thanks."

"I've got to run. I'm late for work."

"'Bye."

"'Bye."

Even this awkward gesture sparked a response. In my rearview mirror I saw Louise showing the bag and note to her friend.

Even after we started to date, I did not get it. One day she had a cake delivered to my house. It came from Mrs. Backer's Bakery, the best of its kind in Salt Lake City, chocolate with chocolate frosting, covered with pink and white flowers. "Happy Unbirthday," the inscription read.

I stood there with the cake in my hands, puzzled over the un-occasion, trying to sort out what this was about. The very fact that I tried to make sense of it, as if it could be justified only by some kind of reason, was symptomatic of later strains we would have. I didn't make the connection at first with *Alice in Wonderland*. No song came into my head, "A very happy unbirthday to you, to you,/ A very happy unbirthday to you . . . " I didn't know that reason could not explain this. It was the madness inside the looking glass.

As I stared at the beautiful cake and its perplexing greeting, my mother came out. "Look what I just got," I said. I held the open cake box out for her to see.

"Who sent you that?" she asked.

"Louise, I think."

"That girl's after you," she said.

I think she meant to warn me, as in, "You'd better watch out, because you have a girl after you and you might fall in love and get married before you get your Ph.D. in eight years and start a career in college teaching."

But I was too caught up in the idea that any girl would

care enough to have Mrs. Backer's deliver a cake to me. I just stared at it. "Happy Unbirthday."

The madness drew me in. This strange girl, who would even get the idea of sending me a cake on one of my 364 unbirthdays, intrigued me. It was so odd, so alien to my practical upbringing, so far from the rational world I had known, where actions had reasons and effects had causes.

It had never occurred to me that birthday cakes were good for any occasion, that you didn't need a birthday to have a celebration. I was to learn from Louise, sometimes reluctantly, to buy a birthday cake to celebrate any possible occasion. One day she brought home a cake because she'd written ten pages. Our boys sang "Happy Birthday to Us" and blew out the candles with gusto. Afterwards, when something nice happened, they would say, "Don't we need a cake?"

I did not realize back then, standing baffled on the porch with a cake in my hands, that I was standing before the looking glass, about to enter Wonderland.

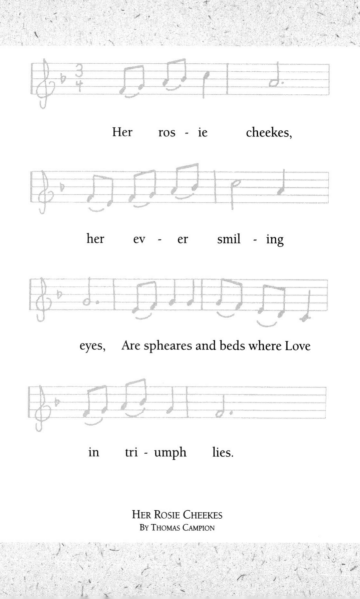

**HER ROSIE CHEEKES**
BY THOMAS CAMPION

# I Married an Aesthete

When I finished my doctorate, Louise and I returned to Cambridge, Massachusetts, for graduation. Dick and Claudia Bushman gave us a reception, inviting our friends from the Boston area. It was a festive occasion, and Louise wanted me to look good. She helped me pick out a new suit and tie.

She took me to a fine men's store, which, she pointed out, was the one and only place to look for a tie. She scanned rack after rack with a critical eye. Finally she held up a bold, red paisley silk number and said, "There. That's truth."

"How much is it?" I asked.

"Never mind. You need this tie," she said. "Buy it."

I looked at the price tag. "I won't pay this much for a tie," I said. "It's a week of groceries."

"We'll eat cake," she said. "Buy the tie."

When we arrived for the open house, Dick met us at the door. He hugged Louise, then took my hand and, with that wry look I had come to know so well, said, "Hi, Tom. I see Louise is still picking out your ties for you."

It had not escaped Dick that a chasm separated me from Louise's aesthetic faculties, although I was just becoming aware of it myself after seven years of marriage. How did he know Louise had picked out my tie? How did he know that she had picked out my ties in years past? Was I such a geek that friends could look at me and know whether I was wearing something I'd chosen or something Louise had chosen for me?

I had only begun to realize that our aesthetic gulf was causing me a great deal of perplexity. I could not have known at the outset that our differences over practicality and beauty would lead to struggles over choices in everything from toasters to toothpaste. Her motivating principle, I finally realized, is simple: If it looks good, it is good. There are two problems with this: First, I am not quite sure what looks good and what doesn't look good; second, what looks good in one moment may not look good in the next. There is, it seems, no sure solution.

*Now I interrupt this essay, because the paradigm of my dilemma just came into the room. It is 7:30 A.M. I got up early, dressed for work, and sat down to write while Louise got ready. I was wearing a tie that Louise had bought for me, an expensive one that I thought would look good with my black blazer and gray pants. Just as I finished the above paragraph Louise entered and said, "You've got on the wrong tie. That one doesn't look good with your blue shirt."*

*"I thought you liked this tie," I said. "You picked it out for me."*

*"No," she said. "Actually I hate the tie. The salesman liked it. I caved in to him."*

*This made me light-headed. As I sat at the computer*

*laughing, Louise said, "I hate you. You're putting that in your book, aren't you?"*

Several corollaries accompany Louise's aesthetic principle:

*Corollary 1: Young is beautiful. Old is ugly.* Nothing is more predictable in our marriage than hearing Louise at the bathroom mirror in the morning, which I have come to think of as her wailing wall. No matter that I think she's beautiful. No matter that other people think she's beautiful. In the morning she stands before the mirror, screws up her face, sticks her tongue out at herself, and wails, "How can you stand it? Look at this turkey neck. Look at the bags under my eyes. I could plant corn in them. Look at my sagging arms. I can wave good-bye with the flab." And she wiggles her raised arms in the morning light to show undulations of aging flesh.

*Corollary 2: Boring is artless and ugly.* A few years ago I was invited to give a fireside presentation to a group of humanities students at the home of Todd and Dorothy Britsch. I saw the occasion as a mixed bag. It was for Brigham Young University students; I was a Brigham

Young University professor. That was the secular side. It was a Sunday-evening fireside; BYU is a church-owned institution. That was the religious side. I decided to talk about some theories of moral development that had caught my attention. That, I thought, combined the sacred and the profane.

I prepared worksheets illustrating, in particular, Lawrence Kohlberg's ideas about morality, and proceeded to conduct a discussion. The students were confused but, in trying to be good sports, participated, making comments way off the mark. We struggled around for some time, and finally I drew a conclusion. There was a closing prayer, "We are grateful for Brother Plummer's presentation," and refreshments. I was not feeling too badly, but Louise was remarkably silent—until we walked into our own living room.

She took a wide swing with her purse, hit me squarely on the shoulder, and said, "That was just awful. You set yourself up as their moral superior, and the whole thing was as dull as dirt. Don't ever do anything like that again."

*Corollary 3: A good car looks good; a bad car looks bad.* There are very few good cars—none of them in our price range. When Renault came out with a convertible, Louise wanted one. I resisted by just acting stupid and keeping my mouth shut, and she finally gave up. VW Beetle convertibles, according to Louise's principle, are good cars. They are the "cutest" cars on the road. Again, I have prevailed only by being passive while agreeing that they are indeed "cute." We never pass one without her sighing deeply. The MG roadster of the 1950s may be one of the most gorgeous cars ever. Fortunately, the only people who own them now are rich folks who have had them restored for enormous sums of money and can afford to own cars that they take out of the garage only on Sundays in the spring, summer, and fall. That doesn't describe us. Of course, there's the Jaguar convertible, the BMW convertible, and the Miata.

"What about the Camry?" I ask. "A good, used one?"

"It's a box. It looks like every other car on the road," she says.

"But it has the highest ratings from consumer magazines," I say.

"Pooh," she says. "What do they know?"

*Corollary 4: A small, beautiful house is better than a big, ugly one.* Recently we moved from a seven-bedroom rambler on the hillside overlooking Utah Valley in Provo to a two-bedroom condominium on the nineteenth floor overlooking Salt Lake City.

Louise was sick of the rambler and yearned for something smaller, something simpler, something more aesthetic. With three sons out of the house and a docile sixteen-year-old left at home, it was possible.

"I'm sick of grass and nature and mountains," she said at least three times a week. "I want concrete. I want cement. Give me New York City or at least Salt Lake City." She would pause, catch her breath, and go on: "I hate this big house. Every closet is full of junk. Two of our seven bedrooms are full of junk. We're wallowing in junk. We need new paint, new drapes, and new carpeting, and we can't afford them."

We had just put our last pennies into replacing a rotting deck outside and a kitchen floor inside. She was right. We were wallowing in junk. We couldn't afford renovations. We sold the house and our treasures, filled a dumpster, and loaded a truck for Deseret Industries. We moved from big to small, from complex to simple, from average to aesthetic.

"I miss trees and grass," Louise said one morning as we sat in our new, perfectly clean condominium overlooking Salt Lake Valley. "I want to step outside and take a breath of air."

"You can step outside," I said. "You go down the elevator nineteen floors and step outside."

"That's not the same," she said. "Don't you ever have the urge just to walk out the door, breathe fresh air, and smell fresh flowers?"

"I don't know," I said. "I was sick of watering the grass, trimming the flowers, and fertilizing the lawn. I haven't thought about those things for a long time. I like this. You wanted small and beautiful. This is small and beautiful. New carpet, new hardwood floors in the kitchen, new black and white tiles in the dining room. It's perfect. What more can you ask?"

"I miss a large dining room," she said. "We can't get our whole family around a table in that little dining room. I miss being matron of the manor. I want to be the matron of the manor again."

"I thought small was better than big," I said. I was being rational and therefore feeling confused. "Do you

want a house again?" I recalled a short poem by A.R.
Ammons:*

> One can't
> have it
>
> both ways
> and both
>
> ways is
> the only
>
> way I
> want it.

"Maybe, maybe not," she said.

*Corollary 5: Real flowers are good. Plastic and silk
flowers are bad.* To that I said, in the early years, if something adds a bit of color and lasts a long time, thus saving
a lot of money, what's so "bad" about that? Huh?

---

*"Coming Right Up," from *The Really Short Poems of A.R. Ammons,* by A. R.
Ammons. Copyright © 1990 by A. R. Ammons. Reprinted by permission of W. W.
Norton & Company, Inc.

"Anybody can see they're phony," Louise would reply.

Eventually I came to see that ficus trees with a lot of hairy stuff around the base were artificial, and even more eventually, I could feel that the texture of the leaves was fabricated. I never developed a visceral repugnance for them, though. It was an intellectual kind of thing. I knew in my head they were "bad," but I didn't feel it in my heart.

Still, I knew right from wrong. That's why, a few years ago, I was so astounded when Louise—repeat, Louise—bought a used, artificial Christmas tree from her sister.

"It doesn't look so bad," she said, "and when I get through decorating it, you won't be able to tell the difference."

Even I could tell the difference. Bits of greenery had fallen off the tree, leaving exposed wires. It was shabby. I thought she was going mad.

"Louise," I said, "have you lost your mind? Can't you see that this fabrication defies all of your aesthetic principles?"

"Oh, it's good to keep you guessing," she said. And she walked away laughing.

December came. Louise was dysfunctional. She lay on

the couch in a fetal position. I asked her if she wanted me to set up the artificial tree.

"No, not yet," she said.

About the tenth of the month, I suggested we get going on the tree. "We have shopping to do, and I don't want to set up the tree at the last minute," I said.

"We'll do it after final exams," she said.

"Louise," I said, becoming exasperated, "we aren't finished with exams until a week before Christmas."

She shrugged and stared out the window. "I don't have the Christmas spirit," she said. "Why don't we skip the tree this year?"

Then I understood. "Come on," I said. "Let's go buy a real tree."

Her eyes brightened. "Really?" she said. "Could we get a real tree? We'll put the artificial one in the family room."

We bought a real tree. We sang Christmas songs as we put on the ornaments: "Silent Night," "Joy to the World," and "Deck the Halls." We never did set up the artificial tree. We gave it back to her sister.

Being married to an aesthete has meant for me a reluctant and painful coming to awareness that beauty may be as important as truth or goodness—that without it, truth and goodness may not be what they're cracked up to be. At the same time, beauty is as evasive as truth and goodness, as slippery as a mermaid. Sometimes you think you have her, and then she's gone, only to return in some other form. I've given up thinking that I'll ever know for sure what's beautiful. Louise worries about this.

"What will you do if I die first?" she asks. "Will you start wearing indestructible polyester pants from K-Mart? Will you know a nice tie when you see one? Will you buy it? Will you remember to zip your fly? Will you check for food in your teeth after you eat? Who will take care of you?"

Frankly, I don't know. I don't worry so much about how I'll look. It's not in my nature. I worry about how I'll feel in the morning not hearing her say, "You're wearing the wrong tie."

Those first sweet vi-o-lets of ear-ly spring, Which

come in whis-pers, thrill us both, and sing of

love un - speakable that    is  to  be—

OH, PROMISE ME
BY CLEMENT SCOTT AND REGINALD DE KOVEN

# Don't Move the Centerpiece

I have not always appreciated the importance of flowers on the table. Not that I grew up with trashy people. My mother prided herself on decorating tables for church and civic lunches and dinners. But watching her haul off dozens of irises, roses, or whatever else was growing in the garden to make tables beautiful made no impression on me. It was women's stuff, and I paid no attention.

Louise changed my thinking, first by example, then by force. Whenever company comes to dinner, she sets the table a full day ahead. For Thanksgiving and Christmas, she sets it two days early. She spreads the white linen tablecloth; irons and sets out linen napkins; positions china, crystal goblets, and sterling silver; and arranges a bouquet of fresh flowers for the centerpiece. The point, she has told me on many occasions, is to present a beautiful setting. The table must meet, if not exceed, the elegance of the meal. Flowers are the crown jewels of the table.

We have many photographs of Louise's table settings. I think of one from our "yellow house," a Georgian colonial. Louise, wearing a red blouse and a black, red, and white apron, stands at the table setting out the china and silverware. Christmas greens and red ribbons adorn the chandelier; a wreath with a substantial red candle in the center decorates the table.

The fact that I even took the picture attests to a change of heart that had begun much earlier, probably on the occasion of our first dinner party. As we sat down with our friends, I noticed that the flowers took up too much space, and we wouldn't be able to fit all the food on the table. Anticipating this problem, I set the centerpiece on the floor with the comment, "These have served their purpose."

Louise gasped and said, "Not the centerpiece."

"There's not enough space," I protested.

"Yes, there is," she said. "Put the centerpiece back on the table and leave it there."

The centerpiece remained on the floor. My position seemed so sensible. If you want to have food on the table, you have to get rid of the centerpiece. If you want to sit and admire the centerpiece, you leave it there and don't eat.

Louise was cheerful with the guests but never looked my way. I waited for the hell I was going to get when they left.

The moment the door shut, she turned on me. "If you ever touch the flowers on the table again, I'll kill you."

"But couldn't you see that the flowers didn't leave any room for the food? And besides," I faltered, "they were obstructing conversation."

"I don't care if they were obstructing your breathing.

Flowers make the table beautiful. That's as important as the food, the conversation, or your breathing."

I now attribute my insensitivity to an obsession with reason. How could the beauty of the table be as important as the meal itself? As the arch-rationalist in the early years of our marriage, I couldn't begin to fathom why people did things that didn't make sense. Flowers on the table didn't make sense. Why flowers? Why not a cage full of puppies? Why not a model train? Why not family photographs? Why not some gerbils? Why not a carton of eggs? What was the point here?

The point, as I was to learn ever so slowly over the next thirty years, was that flowers make a table beautiful. I had married an aesthete, a lover of beauty, a person whose highest value was not how something functioned or tasted, or what social good it accomplished. Of the Greek triad, the Good, the True, and the Beautiful, an aesthete chooses beauty as the highest value. Beauty encompasses both goodness and truth. Without beauty, there is no goodness and no truth.

I argued against this for many years, using every reasonable tactic I had ever learned. Eventually I concluded that this is not a judgment to be reached by reason. To an aesthete, it is a fact. If you don't like it you must either leave, suffer, or die.

I don't know when the turning point came for me. I don't know whether it was an accumulation of flowers, a surrender, or the hope to improve myself—I'd like to think it was the latter—that made me begin to like having flowers on the table. I noticed when other people did not care so much about the table setting. I noticed when flowers made guests happy, when they lightened my own spirits.

At that point I began bringing flowers home on any occasion or non-occasion, because they bring joy to the house. I pick them up at the checkout stand at the grocery store. I stop by neighborhood florists on Friday afternoons so we can have them for the weekend. I do it because I like the flowers. It's a spiritual transformation for me, maybe even an apotheosis. And I never move them from the table.

What dost thou
*E che vo-*

fan - cy can stay one
*le - te che mi con-*

mo-ment So de- spair-ful a
*for - te in co- sì du- ra*

tor-ment, so un-re- lent - ing an-guish?
*sor - te, in co-sì gran mar - ti - re?*

No Longer Let Me Languish
From the opera *Ariana* by Claudio Monteverdi
English translation by Theodore Baker

# Home Improvement

I had never associated home improvement with venereal disease until we bought our first house. It was a narrow, tall structure with white siding, black shutters, and a black roof that rose steeply from the first to the third story. We found it by driving through neighborhoods we liked. It seemed to call to us.

"It looks like a crooked little Dutch house," Louise said. "It's darling." Its slight lean to the south made me nervous, but her clasped hands told me she was charmed.

"But what about the paint on the roof around the dormer?" she asked. "I hate that."

"I can fix that in a jiffy," I said.

"The outside needs paint," she said. The paint on the siding was peeling away in large strips. "Can we paint it?"

"No problem," I said. "I know how to paint a house. I'll just scrape it down, prime it, and put on a new coat."

I went to the door and asked the owner the price.

"Twenty-three thousand, five hundred dollars," she said. That was exactly what we could afford. It was too good to be true.

"Can we just run through?" I asked.

The interior was more intimidating. A filthy, sculpted, yellow carpet from past generations covered the living- and dining-room floors. The walls were scratched and dirty; the kitchen countertop was a worn, dark red linoleum; the carpet was rubber-backed, dirty, mottled red and black. Most bizarre were the stalactites hanging everywhere from the ceilings—plaster spikes, like icicles, one to two inches long. Someone had tried to create a textured surface but had put the plaster on too wet and not wiped it down. The result was stalactites.

"I can knock those off in a couple of hours," I said to Louise, who was quite pale. "I just need a ladder and a scraper."

We made an offer on the spot.

"You have to take care of the ceilings first," Louise said. "I can't live with that for an hour."

I bought a ladder and a couple of scrapers. On the first swipe, the scraper bounced from tip to tip without knocking off a single one. They were hard as granite. I went back to the hardware store, bought heavy-duty scrapers with replacement blades, and swung again. I spent a full week, all day every day, scraping.

After six or seven days, my right elbow swelled to the size of a grapefruit. It was so sore I couldn't stand for even a bedsheet to touch it. My temperature rose to 103 degrees, and I ached all over. I lay in bed moaning. For two days, Louise kept ice packs on me to control the fever.

Finally I called our HMO program. "Dr. Muelleck has an opening tomorrow morning," the receptionist told me.

"Isn't someone available sooner?" I whined. "I want to die."

"Sorry," the voice on the other end said. "Tomorrow

at 9:30 A.M. is the first available appointment. Everyone else is unavailable until next week."

Louise drove me to the clinic the next morning. I groaned all the way there—she has always accused me of having a low pain threshold—and eventually a nurse ushered me into an examination room.

Dr. Muelleck appeared. She was about six-foot-two, sinewy, with straight brown hair, maybe in her forties. With no greeting, she sat down on a stool opposite mine and said, "What's the trouble?" Her tone was cold and cranky. It told me she didn't want to be there.

I pointed to my enormous elbow. "My arm is killing me, and I've had a fever of 103 for three days. I can't eat or sleep."

Her severe expression turned savage. With no warning whatsoever, no hesitation, she took my ailing elbow in both hands and began to squeeze and twist it like she was wringing out a towel. "Does that hurt?" she asked.

I steeled my face to keep my mouth from twitching, although I wanted to writhe on the floor, and said in my coldest, deepest, calmest voice, "Lady, you're killing me."

"Then why aren't you screaming?" she asked.

I could feel sweat breaking out on my forehead. "Because I was taught never to scream in front of a woman," I said.

"Well," she said, recoiling for the next strike. "You've got gonorrhea."

I took a deep breath. "I don't have gonorrhea," I said.

"Yes, you do," she said. "You have gonorrhea."

"Can you get gonorrhea from a toilet seat?" I asked. That much I could remember from my high school health class.

"No, you can't," she said.

"Then I don't have gonorrhea," I said.

"Are you sure?"

"Yes, I'm sure."

"Then you have bursitis," she said.

"What's wrong?" Louise asked when I came out.

"I have gonorrhea," I said.

Once when I was telling this story to a group of friends in Minnesota, Grace Gregory, a woman in her late eighties, said, "I know that doctor. I know her. I took the bus to that very clinic for a physical examination. I was waiting in the little room for my doctor, and this Dr.

Muelleck comes along. Do you know what she said to me? She is not my doctor, but she pokes her head in, sees me, and says, 'You have hardening of the arteries. You'll be dead in six months.' Then she walked off. She didn't even know me. Do you know what I did?"

"What?" I asked.

"Well, in six months, I got on the bus, went all the way across town to that clinic, walked right past the receptionist and down the hall to the examination rooms, and opened every door until I found Dr. Muelleck. She was with a patient. I said, 'You told me six months ago that I'd be dead now. Well, here I am, and I'm not dead.' Then I got on the bus and went home." Grace lived another fifteen years.

Just out of curiosity, I called my old HMO recently to see if Dr. Muelleck was still around. It's been more than twenty-five years since my encounter. "Do you have a Dr. Muelleck on the staff?" I asked.

"Yes, sir," the voice said. "Dr. Muelleck is now at our Fairview Clinic."

Over the years, my rancor toward Dr. Muelleck has receded, not because my heart has softened, but because I have become more grateful for what she did. A more competent doctor would not have given me the story that I so love to tell. Nor would Louise have her favorite opener for times when social conversation slumps: "Tom was diagnosed with gonorrhea."

FLOW GENTLY, SWEET AFTON
BY ROBERT BURNS AND JAMES E. SPILMAN

# There's a Duck in the Chimney

I had not imagined when we bought our first house in Minneapolis with its steeply pitched roof that I would ever deal with that part of its structure. The roof reached from the first to the third floor, creating such a steep pitch that I once got dizzy standing on the ground watching a roofer climb on it. The fireplace was in the middle of the house, so the chimney was dead center on the roofline.

One night we were having a small dinner party with our friends Bill Bracy and Gordon Nebeker. Bill lived in town, but Gordon was flying in from New York. We told Bill just to come in and sit down if we hadn't gotten back from the airport when he arrived.

When Louise and I got home with Gordon, Bill was sitting in the living room looking pale. "There's something in your chimney," he said. He stood up and walked into the dining room.

No sound was coming from the flue, but I thought I'd better take a look before supper just in case. I retrieved a flashlight, crawled into the fireplace on my back, and shone the light up into the chimney. Three or four parallel steel bars formed a grate to separate the chimney from the fireplace. Lying on the grate was something resembling a dead pigeon. It was not stirring, so I figured it posed no immediate problem. I would get it out later.

After dinner we sat in the living room and chatted for a while. No noises emitted from the fireplace. At about ten o'clock Bill went home, Gordon retired to the guest room, and Louise went to bed. I shone the flashlight into the chimney to have another look at the dead pigeon. It was not lying where I had seen it before. Crawling into the fireplace a bit further and moving my face closer to the grate, I shone the flashlight around. The light reflected off two eyes immediately above my face, looking down at me. A long, rounded bill and webbed feet told me the bird was a live duck. I reached up to it. It flapped around in the narrow space. It couldn't fly out, because the chimney went up three stories through the house. Nor could it squeeze down through the narrow bars of the grate.

Recalling from my grade school education that birds eat several times their weight every day—at least that was what I remembered—I tried to give the duck some bread and water. It would have nothing to do with either. It just squawked. I retreated to think about the problem overnight. Maybe I would wake up with a solution.

Just as I got upstairs, our friend Kathy Woolley telephoned Louise, who told her about the duck. Early the next morning Kathy called again. "Listen," she said, "I had a dream last night about how to get the duck out. You put a hose in the chimney, turn on the water full force, and float the duck out."

"Wouldn't that flood the living room?" Louise asked.

"That wasn't in the dream," Kathy said.

Gordon and Louise went shopping and left me to solve the duck problem. The bird was still uninterested in food or water. Our young sons spread the word around the neighborhood that a duck was in the chimney, and smart-aleck neighbors began calling. Why not just start a fire and roast the duck? Would you like a recipe for Peking duck? The more sadistic ones offered strategies for stabbing and dismembering the duck.

I called the Humane Society. They had no means for getting ducks out of chimneys, but wished me luck. The fire department's response was the same. I thought about it all day but came up with nothing. I figured I had twenty-four more hours to come up with a solution before the duck starved. Getting on the roof was not an option. I would not die for a duck.

The next morning I awoke with an idea. I got out my fishing rod and reel, tied a lead sinker on the end of the fishing line, put a ladder up to the house, climbed as high as I could, and began casting to the chimney. Because the ladder reached only to the edge of the roof at the first-story level, I was casting upward for two stories. The line arched over the chimney on the third cast. I reeled slowly back so that when the lead weight dragged over the hole, it would fall in. But the line snagged on the mortar inside the chimney; the weight wasn't heavy enough to pull it down.

I put on a heavier weight and tried again. On the second cast, the line went over the chimney again, and this time, when I dragged it across the hole, it fell all the way into the fireplace.

I went inside, cut the weight off the line, made a knot, and slipped the line over the duck's foot amidst flapping and squawking. I went back out to the ladder and began to reel in. As the line went taut, I realized it was too light to lift the duck. It could break or cut its leg. I retrieved a long clothesline from the basement, cut the fishing line from the duck's foot, and tied the clothesline to the fishing line. Then I returned to the ladder and reeled the clothesline out through the chimney and down to where I could reach it.

That done, I went in and again tied the duck's foot, this time with the heavy clothesline. By now a congregation of neighbors stood on the lawn wisecracking, jeering, and offering more suggestions for foul play. I ignored them and pulled on the rope, slowly and gently. I could feel the dead weight of the duck rising up through the chimney. But when it reached the top, only the foot attached to the rope came out. The duck was upside down. If I pulled too hard from my low angle two stories below, I might break its leg.

I began to lower the duck again, but, seeing the light of day, it flapped its wings and flew out of the chimney. Because the rope was still tied to its foot, it could only fly in big circles over my head, like a model airplane. The neighbors cheered while the duck circled.

In the midst of the jubilation, an old lady, who lived across the street and who had been unaware of the proceedings, came running out of her house yelling at me, "What are you doing with that duck? What are you doing with that duck?" The neighbors calmed her down and explained that I had just fished the duck out of the chimney and saved its life. She joined in the cheering.

The duck finally landed on the lawn, but before I could reach it, Louise rushed out of the house—this is the honest truth—with broken bread and water on our best china. I think she wanted it to sit down and have a formal dinner before leaving. The ungrateful duck flapped its wings and tried to get away. I slipped the rope from its foot and it flew off toward nearby Lake Nokomis.

O Dry Those Tears!
By Teresa del Riego

# Thumb Sucking

When I asked our son Charles, then five, why he sucked his thumb, he said, without hesitating and without taking his thumb out of his mouth, "I'm punishing you." Saliva ran down his thumb, over his chin, and onto his pants as he spoke.

I had not expected this answer. I suppose now, in thinking about it, I expected, "I don't know," or, "Because I like to." It was not a question I thought he would answer so astutely. I might have reasoned that he sucked his thumb because he had done it in the womb—you see pictures of prenascent babies doing this—and had gotten the habit there. Or I could have thought this was a psychological replacement for nursing or fulfillment of an Oedipal need. The last thing I had expected was, "I'm punishing you."

"Why are you punishing me?" I asked. "Are you mad at me?"

But he just rolled his eyes toward me and stared, the way Charles often did.

Charles was the second of our four sons to suck his thumb. His older brother, Ed, had persisted until he was ten. The problem is that thumb sucking applies pressure to the lower jaw, which retards its development and results in an overbite. Ed had to have jaw surgery to correct the problems his thumb sucking had caused. By the time Charles was six, his lower jaw was showing the same underdevelopment as Ed's.

Of equal concern to us was that Charles's thumb sucking had begun to affect his schoolwork. He is right-handed, and he sucked his right thumb. He tried to write with his left hand so he could keep his thumb in his mouth. His teacher showed us his futile scribblings. Moreover, his thumb had become so raw and painful that he could no longer even hold a pencil in his right hand. Our various attempts to bribe him to keep his thumb out of his mouth at school had failed.

I became obsessed with stopping the habit. I put Tabasco sauce on his thumb. That made it burn and he howled while I washed it off, apologizing. I wrapped it in bandages and put Tabasco sauce on the bandages. He took the bandages off and kept sucking. I threatened. I cajoled. To no avail.

Saturday mornings in those years were the time for cleaning rooms. On one particular Saturday, Charles was dawdling around and whining to go out with his friends.

"Charles," I said, "first you have to clean your room. If you don't want to clean your room, you can sit here on the stairs and think about cleaning your room until you are ready to finish the job. You aren't going out until you're done."

Charles sat down on the stairs and jammed his thumb into his mouth. *He's punishing me,* I thought.

I had been reading the biography of a psychologist by

the name of Milton Erickson who had had considerable success with patients suffering from obsessive-compulsive behavioral patterns. One of his strategies was to push the obsessive behavior to the extreme, thus forcing the obsessor to face the ultimate consequences.

This spawned an idea. I went to the bedroom, where Louise was working, and shared it with her. "We both have to be committed to this, or it won't work," I said. "Are you game?"

"Yes. It's worth a try," she said.

I went back to Charles and sat on the stairs by him. "Charles," I said, "I've been thinking about things you do well. You are really smart. You can read and write, you can play the violin, you have nice friends. But do you know what I think you do best?"

He rolled his eyes up to mine while he rested his right elbow on the stairs and sucked his thumb.

"Thwat?" he asked through slobber.

"Thumb sucking. Charles, you do that better than anything else. You do that better than anyone I know. You could become a professional thumb sucker. You could make a fortune sucking your thumb in circus sideshows.

I can see the sign: 'World's Best Thumb Sucker Here.' But you know what, Charles," I went on, "you're not professional enough. You just stick your thumb in your mouth like this." I put my thumb limply in my mouth. "But professional thumb suckers really go at it. They smack their lips on their thumbs like this." I popped my lips on my thumb hard and loud. "I think for the next few days you should practice being a professional thumb sucker. I want you to practice a half hour every day and see if you've got what it takes."

Charles jerked his thumb out of his mouth. "No way," he yelled. "I ain't suckin' my thumb. The dentist said suckin' your thumb is bad for you. No way."

"Oh, professional thumb suckers don't even care about dentists," I said. "Dentists want people to have nice, even teeth. Professional thumb suckers have their teeth sticking straight out from their mouth. That's how people know they are professional thumb suckers." I extended my fingers straight from my mouth to suggest how teeth should be perpendicular to the gums. "You won't ever have to go the dentist again. He'll just want to fix your teeth."

By now Jon and Ed had come out of their rooms, curious about what was happening. They stood at the head of the stairs watching their helpless brother.

"Yes, Charles," I persisted in a calm voice. "We are going to see if professional thumb sucking is for you. Now I am going to set the oven timer for thirty minutes. During that time you are going to suck your thumb hard." I popped my lips on my thumb to demonstrate. "And if you take your thumb out during that thirty minutes, or if the sucking gets wimpy, I will reset the timer, and you will have to start over."

"Mom," Charles yelled with his thumb in his mouth. "Call the police and tell them Dad's making me suck my thumb."

"Remember, Charles," I said. "Don't take your thumb out during this half hour. What's more, if I see you sucking your thumb the rest of the day, I'll assume it means you want another practice session, and we'll have it right on the spot. You are in charge here."

I went into the bedroom and shared a smothered laugh with Louise while the baffled older brothers gaped at Charles sucking and wailing.

"Keep those lips smacking on that thumb," I yelled from the bedroom. "I can't hear you."

That night, as Charles climbed into bed, I asked what he planned to do with his thumb while he was asleep. This brought a new barrage of objections. "I can't keep my thumb out of my mouth while I'm sleeping," he hollered. "It's like smoking. You can't just quit all of a sudden."

I wasn't sure how he knew about smoking, but I persisted. "Charles, if I come in and you're sucking your thumb, we'll have an extra practice session tomorrow. It's up to you."

He sat in bed for a while thinking. Then he went to his closet, pulled out a pair of mittens, and asked me to tape them to his arms.

The next day, Sunday, Charles slipped once. He spent an extra half hour with the oven timer. By Monday, it was all over. He asked to skip practice. "I don't want to be a professional thumb sucker," he said. "It's too much work."

"Okay," I said. "Let me know if you ever want to try it again. I'll bet thumb suckers make a lot of money."

BILLY BOY
TRADITIONAL

# Chocolate-Chip Cookies for Dinner

This is how I began cooking: Our church services lasted from 9:00 A.M. to 12:00 noon each Sunday. By the time we arrived home, around 12:30 or 1:00 P.M., our four boys were ravenous. This manifested itself in uncivilized ways. Number-one son would beat up on number-two son, who would whine and suck his thumb and slobber. Then number-one son would move to number-three son, who would try to fight him, in spite of the fact that he was five years junior and thirty pounds lighter. Then number-one son would move to number-four son, snatch his bottle, and hide it. Within five minutes of walking through the door everyone was slugging, whining, slobbering, yowling.

"I'll make chocolate-chip cookies for dinner if you'll all just be quiet," Louise shouted one day over the delirium.

My stomach clenched. Louise, it seemed to me, had made a decision born of desperation. Chocolate-chip cookies, eclairs, and ice cream are fine as desserts, but they must not be the main course. You do not feed growing boys chocolate-chip cookies for the most important meal of the week.

But they cheered as she whipped up some cookie dough and tossed it in the oven. "Are you planning on a real meal later?" I asked.

"This is a real meal," she said.

The boys cleaned up a double batch of cookies and a gallon of milk, said thank you very much, Mom, that was good, and settled down to some TV and games.

The next Sunday on the way to church, Ed, the

eternally hungry one, asked, "Mom, can we have choco-late-chip cookies for dinner?"

"You bet," she said. "I bought more chocolate chips this week."

After dinner, when we were alone—at least I'd like to think I waited that long—I said to her, "Louise, we can't keep having chocolate-chip cookies for dinner. We need meat and vegetables and salad and fruit. These are grow-ing boys. I can feel my blood thicken. I'll die before my time."

"Cookies are good for you. They heal you," she said. "I don't care if I ever eat vegetables again."

"Then I'm taking over Sunday dinners," I said.

"That's fine," she replied. "Go for it."

That very week I bought a recipe book called *More Wok Cookery.* I planned the first meal, "South-African Lamb Pilaf," and shopped for the ingredients we didn't have in the cupboard: dried apples, pitted prunes, raisins, lean lamb, bread crumbs, red-wine vinegar, and bulgur. The bulgur took the longest to find, because I had not the faintest idea what it was.

"Mom, can we have chocolate-chip cookies for dinner?" Ed asked the next Sunday on the way to church.

"Your dad's fixing dinner today," she said.

"What're we having, Dad?" he asked.

"It's a surprise," I said.

After church the usual howling began—now that cookies weren't on the menu—but I was too caught up in fixing the meal to pay attention. Louise slipped off to the bedroom to watch TV, nap, and wait for dinner. I combined apples, prunes, and raisins in a large bowl. I mixed lamb, bread crumbs, milk, egg, salt, and paprika. I rolled meatballs, fried them, and began the stir-fry. When I put in the curry powder, Charles howled about the awful stench. When I added the fruits, vinegar, and sugar, Jon began to yuk it up. "Fruit and meat? That's icky," he yelled, and popped Ed on the head.

When I spooned the bulgur onto a platter, topped it with the lamb mixture, garnished it with banana slices, and sprinkled peanuts over it, they all paled. "Call your mom," I said. "We're ready to eat."

Louise and I wolfed down our portions. "This is great," she said, taking another helping of meatballs. The boys picked around, ate a bit of the meat, complained about the weird taste of curry, and left the rest. I ignored them and saved the leftovers.

"Next Sunday, we'll have another delicious meal," I said.

"Yes, mastuh," Jonathan said as he pushed off from the table.

On the same page as the "South-African Lamb Pilaf" was a recipe for "Couscous with Lamb and Apricots," a North African dish. Culturally, I decided we would work our way north from South Africa to Norway. I would not only feed them, I'd teach them. Maybe I'd write an essay on feeding as an educational enterprise.

On Friday, I picked up the lean lamb, dried apricots, slivered almonds, and couscous, which I eventually found near the bulgur. As I shopped, I held an imaginary conversation with Louise. "Sunday meals must be well planned and executed," I told her in my head. "They must set an example for a lifetime. They must instruct." In my fantasy, she nodded in agreement.

"Mom, can we *please* have chocolate-chip cookies for dinner today?" Ed asked on the way to church.

"No, your dad's in charge of Sunday meals," she said. Her tone was wry. "I'm sure he's planning something very healthy today." It seemed to me she said "healthy" with a slightly sarcastic, disparaging tone.

After church, Louise retired to the bedroom while the boys engaged in mortal combat. I focused my attention on the meal. I stir-fried onion, added lamb, spooned off fat, added apricots, almonds, water, butter, and salt. I stirred in the couscous until the liquid was absorbed and announced that dinner was ready.

"What is it?" Charles asked.

"It's couscous with lamb and apricots," I said proudly.

"What's that?" he persisted.

"It's a North-African dish," I said, pleased to educate them with both cultural and culinary experiences.

Charles went ballistic: "Can't we just have some good old American hamburgers?"

Slightly wounded, I served the food. Even Louise, the aesthetic advisor, said it looked lovely. It was the taste of apricots that got them.

"Geez, this is awful," Ed said. He was gagging and spitting food back onto his plate. This was particularly painful, because Ed was the one kid who could eat almost anything. "What are these little orange things?"

"Dried apricots," I said.

"They taste a little dusty," Louise said.

"They're sour," Jon said. "Ucky."

Most of the meal went down the disposal. I ate my portion to prove that the hollering was unjustified, but I didn't complain that they were throwing theirs away. I kept no leftovers.

The next Sunday I served chocolate waffles. No one complained about the absence of fruit and vegetables. No one wondered aloud what had happened to my culinary education project. Louise had a smirk on her face during dinner.

To this day, when the discussion of food comes up in family gatherings, there is no mercy. "Do you remember when Dad made couscous with lamb and apricots? Gag me." They all writhe and retch like they are reliving the experience.

Louise smiles and awaits the next line: "But do you remember when Mom made chocolate-chip cookies for Sunday dinners? That was awesome."

She was happy till she met you, and the

fault is all your own, If she

wish-es   to   for - get you,   you will

please let   her   a - lone.

SHE WAS HAPPY TILL SHE MET YOU
BY CHAS GRAHAM AND MONROE H. ROSENFELD

# Practicing Diplomacy

I read once that almost every married couple renegotiates the terms of their marriage between years twelve and eighteen. It's as predictable as wrinkled skin. This is not necessarily a formal negotiation, in which people sit down and plot out the next ten or fifty years, although it could be. It is more commonly something that happens without people realizing it.

It comes with the pressures of midlife, when the conditions of marriage and family bring about changes in situation and attitude. Couples become bored with each other. The early physical attractions have waned a bit. Wrinkles and bumps have appeared in unattractive places. Teenagers and younger children alike, demanding to be chauffeured, paid, and honored, divide their parents' attention and affections. Money tightens as cars, food, education, and clothing compete for limited resources.

For many couples, the twelve-to-eighteen stretch is too hard. They get divorced. Others stay together but "plateau out," giving up any hope of a passionate or even interesting marriage in advanced years. Still other couples work out new terms, new understandings about the original premises of their vows, and go on to more exciting things.

One evening in those dark twelve-to-eighteen years, we were renegotiating the terms of our marriage, and it looked bleak. I was wearing my wool suit pants, white shirt, and a tie. I must have come from a late meeting. Louise and I were in our bedroom talking about intense and nervous stuff. Maybe it was about disciplining one of the kids. Maybe it was about money. I don't remember. We had several sore spots that could precipitate a crisis.

I probably said something like, "Well, if you'd handled it differently, we wouldn't be in this spot."

She jumped to her feet. "If you'd been here to help, you big jerk, we wouldn't be in this spot. You expect me to carry the whole ball. Where are you?" She was raging. Velociraptors have nothing on Louise's rage. She stormed out of the bedroom, slammed the door, and rushed down the hall.

I jumped up and followed. "Louise, come on. I'm sorry. Don't run off." My voice had a pleading, whining tone. It does that when I commit a foul. I've never been able to bluff it.

"Don't follow me, you creep. Get out and leave me alone."

She stormed down the stairs with me in pursuit. "C'mon, honey," I said. "I'm sorry."

"Don't call me honey," she yelled. "I'm not your little honey. I'm not your little fix-it girl. Beat it."

I wouldn't back off, and she roared through the living room, dining room, and kitchen with me chasing her. I grabbed her arm; she jerked it away and shoved me off. She headed back up the stairs, through the bedroom, the original scene of the fight, and into the adjoining bathroom, yelling, "Leave me alone! Just leave me alone!"

She slammed the door and locked it. I could hear the bathwater running. Louise takes baths when she is miserable.

I was sickened. I knocked on the door. "Louise," I said, "I'm really sorry. I was an insensitive clod. Please forgive me." My tone fell short of genuine remorse—I was trying to get out of trouble. No response. The bathwater was still running. I knocked again. "Louise, please," I said.

"Get out of here and leave me alone. Just go away," she yelled. "I'm taking a bath."

I became desperate. Rushing to the workshop, I found a screwdriver and returned to the bathroom door. I unscrewed the bolt on the knob, then the screws on the facing plate. The workings of the lock were now exposed, and I could see how to get inside.

"If you come in here, I'll kill you," she hollered.

"I'm coming in," I said. I pried the latch apart and opened the door.

"Get out of here," she yelled. "Get out."

"We have to talk," I said. I was trying to be cool, but I could feel panic throbbing in my chest.

"We're not talking. Get out." She was practically snarling through bared teeth.

I got a chair and set it by the bathtub. She hurled a dripping washrag on it so I couldn't sit down. I put the rag back in the tub. She smashed it back on the chair.

I looked at her. She glared at me. Then I climbed into the bathtub, wool pants, shirt, tie, dress shoes, and all and sat down facing her.

She started to laugh. She laughed for a long time. I was confused. I thought we were at war. Was she laughing at me? Then she reached out with both wet arms and hugged me. I hugged her back, relieved but perplexed.

"You hurt my feelings," she said. "It's against the rules to hurt my feelings."

"I know," I said. "Will you please forgive me?" This time my tone was right.

"Yes," she said. "I love you. But don't hurt my feelings ever again."

"I won't," I said. "I'm sorry. I really am sorry."

We sat in the tub together for a while. Louise seemed

mellow; I was sober, subdued. Our boys were in the bedroom when I walked out, still dressed, dripping water all over the floor. They looked at me like I was a drunken sailor. "Don't ask," I said. "And if you ask, I can't tell you. I don't know."

Will you   love me in De - cember  as you

do    in   May? Will you

love me   in the good old-fash-ioned  way?

**WILL YOU LOVE ME IN DECEMBER AS YOU DO IN MAY?**
BY JAMES J. WALKER AND ERNEST R. BALL

# Snowblowing

For me, necessity is the mother of small business enterprise. I am no businessman. I am a business moron, even though I have dreamed for years of having my own small business. My opportunities to be an entrepreneur have generally arisen out of desperation—when we have been broke.

Such an opportunity arose in the summer of 1982, when we moved into a new house in St. Paul, Minnesota. It cost more than we could afford, and so I told the family after moving in that we would have to cut unnecessary expenses. In my mind that was clothes, trips to Baskin-Robbins, allowances, and spending money for the boys.

"Did you plan a budget without clothes, allowances, and treats? Are you telling me that you said we could afford this house but that you left essentials out of the budget?" Louise asked when I made my announcement. She locked me into her radar and prepared to fire. "How about cutting trips to your favorite haunts?"

"Like what?" I said. "I don't spend extra money."

"Oh, give me a break," she said. "How about that VCR you bought for $900? You could have gotten one for $400 and bought clothes all around with the balance."

"I needed a good one," I said. I could feel my eye twitch. "I needed one with four heads and special-effects stuff. Professional expenses. You know that."

"Professional expenses, my foot," she said. "You just like to go first class. You aren't going to take this out of everyone else's hide. That isn't fair and you know it."

"Well, how about if I help the boys earn some money?" I asked. "Is that all right with you?"

"As long as you take your turn with them," she said. "Don't just stick them with your problem. And don't stick me with it either. I'm going to buy clothes when I need them. You weren't being straight about the budget. Come on, boys," she yelled, "Dad's taking us all to Baskin-Robbins. It's treat time."

That was in July. By October, pressure was mounting. The older boys were in their teen years; personal and school expenses were up. They were too young to work, and I couldn't bankroll them and the rest of the budget.

Over dinner one evening Ed hit me for ten dollars for a youth party at church. I exploded. "If every guy in the family asked me for ten dollars every week, that would be forty dollars a week, a hundred and sixty dollars a month. You don't think that way, do you? You don't think about the needs of the whole family?" Ed sat there stunned.

Louise cut in. "Here's ten dollars from your dad's birthday money," she said, handing Ed a bill. "Have a good time." Ed skipped out and she turned on me. "You have to figure this out," she said. "You can't make them responsible for our budget. What did you think you were going to do? Tell him he couldn't go to a church party, for pity's sake?"

I held to the notion that they too had to be responsible.

I picked up the want ads to see what ideas might reveal themselves. The help-wanted section was useless. Accountants, dental technicians, electricians, plumbers, nothing for us. Nothing for a German professor and three boys. I rambled on through the ads. "Snowblowers and snow removal equipment." I paused there. One ad read, "Snowblower, 5 hp, good condition. $100."

"Hey, what about snowblowing?" I yelled to Louise. "I could start a snowblowing business with Jon and Ed. How about that? No problem with snow around here, and I'll bet people would appreciate the service."

"Fine," she called back. "Just be sure you're involved too."

I went off to see the snowblower. A guy pulled a hunk of ancient equipment out of his garage. Red and white, covered with rust spots.

"Does it run?" I asked.

"Like a charm," he said. He pulled the cord, and the mighty engine started up. The whole thing shook like it was going to fall apart.

"How do you make the blades turn?" I shouted over the din.

"Just push on this lever," he said. He slammed it with his hand, and the blades kicked into gear.

"How about eighty dollars and I take it off your hands?" I asked as he shut it down.

"Nope," he said. "Three other people are on their way. Rock-bottom price is one hundred dollars."

I forked over five twenties, and he helped me lift it into the Escort station wagon. "By the way," he said, "do you know about shear pins?"

"No," I said. I had no idea what he was talking about.

"Well, snowblowers have shear pins to hold the blades in place. If you hit a big chunk of ice or something, the shear pins break so the blades will stop turning and the machine doesn't self-destruct. See, here's a shear pin." He pointed to what looked like a large nail on the steel shaft holding the blades. "And here's the other one. Stop at a hardware store and pick up a handful of them, because you'll need them."

*I'll just be careful*, I thought to myself. *He probably ran into big chunks of ice because he was careless.* I hummed on the way home: "Sleigh bells ring, are you listening? La dee da, la dee da da . . . Let it snow, let it snow, let it snow."

"Hi, Ed," I called as he walked in from his party. "Hey, Jon, you guys come in here. I've got something to tell you." Ed was cautious. I assumed it was because I'd bitten his head off earlier. Jon was always cautious. They came into the living room. "Sit down here," I said. "Listen, you guys, how'd you like to have some extra money to spend this winter? Wouldn't it be nice to have a little cash you can use for things like church parties?"

"I can get that from Mom," Jon said.

"Yeah," I said trying to keep cool, "but I mean, wouldn't it be nice to know you'd earned the money yourself? Wouldn't that give you a feeling of satisfaction? Like being a grown-up?"

"Get to the point," Louise yelled from the kitchen.

"I bought a snowblower tonight," I said. "We're going to have a little snowblowing business this winter so you guys don't have to hit me up for money all the time. I'll help you, but you are going out to blow snow off people's walks for money."

"I saw the new Honda ads on TV," Ed said. "They throw the snow a mile."

"I didn't buy a Honda," I said.

"A Toro?" Jon said. "They start with one pull."

"No," I said. "I don't know what kind this is. It's used, and you can't see the label anymore. It's out in the garage. Come on."

With the thrill of new and powerful equipment driven from their minds, they shuffled into the garage to see what I had.

"No way. That's a piece of junk," Jon said. "I ain't doin' no snowblowin' with that."

"If you want any money for the rest of the winter, you are," I said. "From now on, you earn your keep. One of you can use this one, and one can use the old electric one hanging over there." I pointed to a battered electric snow remover I'd bought from another professor once. "You can trade off. Now, here's what we're going to do. We'll make up some flyers, and you take them around the neighborhood. We'll offer people a snowblowing contract, $75 for the winter. If we get ten contracts, that's $650 that's yours. I pay for the blower with the first $100."

"So if we get a hundred contracts, we get $7,500?" Ed asked.

"That's $7,400," I said. "I get $100 for the blower, remember."

That last figure made a convert of Jon. "Let's make up the flyers," he said.

We printed 150 flyers, and the boys took them to neighbors. This was mid-October. The leaves are barely off the trees in Minnesota by then, and the sense of urgency has not kicked in among the general population. The signs of winter are just emerging. Snow usually falls around Thanksgiving. Consequently, only three people signed on. Still, I put the $100 for the snowblower back in the bank and set $125 aside for church parties and the like for the boys.

"Give them each ten dollars for passing out those flyers," Louise demanded. "They have to have some reward for working besides just keeping you happy." I grudgingly forked over twenty dollars and the boys headed out for Speedy Market down the hill.

Minnesota is a funny place in the fall. Temperatures often drop below freezing, but skies remain blue, and there's little sign that full-blown blizzards are on their way. It's the kind of place that veterans take seriously. They have their cars tuned by late October—new spark plugs, lightweight oil, good snow tires—because they know that when the first snowstorm hits, it's too late. Within hours after a few inches or feet, depending on the winter, the temperature drops to twenty below and everything in sight turns to ice. Cars freeze in place on the ground, and any vehicle not properly prepared for winter just doesn't start again until spring—if then.

The winter of snowblowing was probably my twelfth in Minnesota. I was a veteran. But I was not prepared for the much darker than usual cloud cover and fierce winds that I woke up to the day after Thanksgiving. On the television, forecasters were announcing a major winter storm.

While we were eating breakfast, the doorbell rang. Three neighbors were standing on the porch. All had come to the same conclusion—they needed snowblowing contracts for the winter. I looked at the sky and then at their desperate eyes and said, "Sorry, guys, we've got all the work we can handle." They whined. One claimed he had a heart condition. I sent them on their way.

By noon it was snowing hard, and it didn't stop until eighteen inches had fallen. I found Ed and Jon staring out the window in a semicomatose state. "Come on, guys," I said, "we've got work to do. Come on, before it gets so cold we can't work."

"The weatherman says it's already below zero," Jon said.

"Yeah, we'll die out there," Ed chimed in.

"Get your coats and boots on," I yelled from the garage. "The longer we wait, the worse it will be."

I cranked up the beast and hit the wall of snow on the other side of the garage door. The engine groaned, slowed way down, and then threw snow out the chute. Filled with hope, I did two or three laps before I hit a bump. The blades quit turning. I had broken a shear pin. I looked at the shaft, which was now covered with snow and ice, hardening with every second in the freezing air. I had no shear pins. Jon and Ed were now trudging out of the garage.

"You can go inside for a bit," I yelled from the snowblower. "I've got to buy some shear pins." They cheered and retreated. Fortunately, the hardware store had shear pins and ice picks. I bought some of each.

At home again, I chipped the ice off the shank, put in new shear pins, which I could hold only with bare hands, retrieved Jon and Ed, and tried to ease the pain of my frozen hands by holding them under my arms. I cranked up the big machine and turned it over to Jon. Then I got Ed started with the electric machine. We still had not gotten beyond our own house, and we had hours of work ahead.

Louise called out the door. "The woman down the street says she has a snow removal contract and wants to know when you're coming."

"Tell her she's next," I hollered. "The twelfth of never," I muttered under my breath. At that moment the city plow came by and filled our newly cleared driveway with a four-foot wall of ice and snow. I stood on the curb shaking my fist and yelling at the driver, who smiled and waved.

Six hours and six shear pins later, the jobs were all done. The boys stood in the house yelling that their hands and feet were frozen. Mine hurt too, but I tried not to yell. Louise served hot soup.

That was the first day of a record-setting winter for snowfall in Minnesota. By Christmas, we had forty-eight inches on the ground. Every time it began to snow, the boys would start to cry. After two or three snowfalls, I had to bribe them to go out with me—first five dollars, then ten apiece. Some nights I was out in a neighbor's driveway cursing the shear pins with my gloves off at twenty below while the boys were at a church party. By the time the last snow came in March, ninety-six inches had fallen, and I had bankrolled the project for several hundred dollars more than we had gotten in contracts.

"What on earth made you think of snowblowing?" Louise asked one night as we lay in bed reminiscing. "Didn't you remember how much it snows in Minnesota?"

"Well, that's precisely the point," I said. "There's a clear need. Snow makes the need obvious. If we'd had some real equipment, maybe it would have worked."

"You're an idiot," she said. "You're saying if you'd spent a thousand dollars more you could have earned more money. You'd have been out there longer than you were. I have some advice for you," she said.

"What's that?"

"Don't ever go into business. You don't know how to do it." She took my hand. "You're a German professor. Live with it."

Work, for the night is    com - ing,

Work thru the morning   hours.

WORK, FOR THE NIGHT IS COMING
BY ANNIE L. WALKER-COGHILL AND LOWELL MASON

# Master Seal Coaters

We used to rely on my summer teaching for money to get through July, August, and September. Teaching is all German professors can do for money. No one wants them as business consultants. No one wants them to save the ozone layer. In the summer of 1983, there was no teaching available. *Nada. Nichts.* I could not imagine how we would get the money we needed for the summer.

"Oh, get a grip," Louise said as I sat on the sofa in a funk. "There must be something. You've got five weeks before school ends."

Meanwhile, our asphalt driveway was cracking, and mini-potholes were beginning to appear. In Minnesota you can't ignore damaged asphalt, because water seeps into the holes and cracks, freezes with the winter cold, expands, and *voilà:* asphalt jungle in the spring. Another year, and we would have to replace the entire driveway.

Although spending any money at all made me retch, I went to a hardware store and asked what I had to do to seal the surface. A clerk showed me five-gallon cans of seal coat—a coal tar compound with the consistency of heavy latex—tubes of crack sealer, a sealant to cover oil spots, a push broom, and a squeegee, which was a fifteen-inch-wide rubber blade mounted on a broom handle.

"There are some important tricks here," he said. "First, the driveway has to be absolutely clean. Sweep it, then hose it down, then get a big bucket of soapy water and scrub the oil spots with the broom. Rinse it, then brush the blue sealant over the oil spots and let it dry. Fill the cracks with crack sealer and let that dry. When that's done, stir the seal coat in the five-gallon can. It has about twenty pounds of sand in it. You have to blend the mixture. Do you follow me?"

I nodded stupidly.

"Then spray just enough water on the driveway to dampen it, so the coal tar spreads easily. Pour out a little coal tar at a time, and use the squeegee to spread it around evenly. Don't forget to keep mixing the coal tar. The sand will sink back to the bottom." I shifted from one foot to the other. "One last thing," he said. "You cannot apply this if it's going to rain or if the temperature will drop below forty-five degrees before it's dry. It will all wash or flake off, and you'll have coal tar everywhere. Oh, yeah," he continued, "one other thing. If you get it on something and it dries, you can only remove it by sand-blasting." He rambled on in a pleasant voice, like a doctor who is about to hurt you: "Oh, yeah. I almost forgot. Don't wear clothes you can't throw away. This stuff doesn't wash out."

He cheerfully helped me load the car. "Good luck," he yelled as I pulled away. It sounded like a threat.

I got home around noon. The temperature was in the 80s, with only a puffy cloud or two in the sky. I put on the oldest pants, shoes, and shirt I could find, hooked up the hose, washed down the driveway, filled a bucket with water and dish soap, and began to scrub the oil spots. They scarcely changed. I hit them again. And again. After half a dozen passes, they faded a bit.

I spread the sealer on the oil spots, opened a tube of crack filler, got about halfway along one crack, and ran out. Two tubes left, at three dollars a tube. It was all gone before I had finished one-quarter of the driveway. I rushed to the hardware store, bought eight more tubes, and finished filling the cracks.

I was ready for the coal tar. I broke off a couple of small boards trying to stir up the sand in the bottom of the bucket. I got a two-by-four. The sand gave way grudgingly. The coal tar on top ran over the rim. The board slipped. Tar flew up and hit my glasses. *Just keep going,* I thought. Another slip. It was on my shirt and pants. I stirred for fifteen or twenty minutes before I had a uniform texture.

I poured some on the driveway, and it thickened almost instantly. I had forgotten to spray the asphalt with water. I scrambled for the hose and sprayed on too much. The coal tar ran down the driveway toward the sidewalk, which, I remembered, would turn permanently black. I grabbed the squeegee and headed off the stream just as it reached the concrete.

Eventually I got it right. Spray on a fine mist, pour out coal tar, squeegee. About halfway through the job, the idea hit me that other people would pay a lot to have someone do this for them. I could be that someone. By now I had coal tar on my face, my arms, my glasses, my shirt, my pants, and my shoes. I was on my way to becoming a professional seal coater.

I discovered during cleanup that soap and water would not remove the dried seal coat from my skin. I needed bug-and-tar remover from the local auto supply store. Using soaked rags, I carefully removed the sandy-textured tar from arms, face, neck, hair, and glasses. I smelled like a chemical plant. I tossed the clothes in a corner of the garage and walked into the house amidst complaints from the entire peanut gallery about the smell.

The next morning I looked up "Asphalt and Asphalt Products" in the Yellow Pages. Two companies sold seal-coat products wholesale. I called Coal Tar, Inc. "Do you sell to contractors?" I asked.

"You bet," the guy on the other end said. He sounded friendly, encouraging. "Are you a contractor?"

"Look," I said, "I'm a university professor, but this summer I need money. Can I hope to make any money in a seal-coating business?"

"Oh, yeah," he said. "I have a lot of teachers buying from me. I can get you started. I have all the commercial equipment. Why don't you come out and we'll talk. You can do this."

In fifteen minutes I was in the car, headed for an industrial part of town, far from universities and intellectuals, light years from libraries, theaters, and museums. I found Coal Tar, Inc., in a big warehouse, the kind I'd seen in chase scenes in the movies. A burly guy named Max ushered me into his office. He fired his opener: "I have a contractor who makes $80,000 a summer doing this. He spends winters in Florida. Of course," he went on, "he has a lot of equipment—trucks, coal-tar sprayers, a real operation. How much are you willing to invest?"

"I'm almost broke," I said. "I have to do this on a shoestring."

"Well," he said, "some guys are working out of the

back of their cars. They buy five-gallon buckets of seal coat and go to work. I don't recommend it. You pay a premium price for the material and you mess up your car. But it's a start. You'll need a blower with an eight-horsepower engine, that's $550, some thirty-inch squeegees, not those dinky things you buy at hardware stores," he spread his arms to suggest the width, "some buckets of coal tar that cost half as much as you paid, a bucket of crack sealer, not like the tubes you bought, and several gallons of sealer to spread on oil spots. I think we can get you going for about $700."

"Do you take Visa?" I asked.

"Yup," he said.

"I'll think it over," I said. I hadn't anticipated this industrial-strength approach. But by the time I got home I was ready. Over dinner I made the announcement. "We're going into the seal-coating business," I said in a power voice. "I've been out to a wholesaler, and I can get supplies and equipment to get started."

"How much does that cost?" Louise asked.

"About $700," I said.

She kept silent for a minute or two. "Is that all you're going to need?" she asked.

"Well, that's the basic equipment and supplies," I said. "I can work out of the Escort."

"So you don't need a truck or something awful like that?" she persisted.

"Not for the time being," I said. "We'll just see first how it goes."

She whooped. "You're going to be a blue-collar worker. I'm going to call my mother right now and ask if she'll give you my father's old lunch bucket. He hasn't used it since he retired. I love it." I was fully unprepared for this reaction. I had not realized the respect she had for a man who worked with his hands. In her eyes I was entering the real work force.

"What're you going to call the company?" Charles asked.

"Master Seal Coaters," I said.

Louise snorted. "Master Seal Coaters? You're no master."

"I figure after you do your own driveway you're a master," I said. I turned to Ed, then thirteen. "You're going to help me. This is a family business. I'll pay you a dollar an hour."

"Can't I have two dollars an hour?" he asked.

"Nope," I replied. "A dollar an hour is all I can afford."

I ignored Louise's glare. Besides, she was already shopping for work clothes in her head. "You'll need some bib overalls," she said, "some good work shirts, and—"

"Look," I said, "this is grimy stuff. Everything gets covered with tar. I'm putting on the oldest clothes I have. By the end of the first day, they won't be worth anything."

"But you'll look like a dork," she said.

"Yeah."

She quashed her disappointment. She was calling her mother as I left the room.

The next morning I went back to Coal Tar, Inc., laid down my Visa card, and bought all the accoutrements of my new trade. As I crammed them into the car, I knew I needed a truck. I would go for it after a job or two.

I opened a business account at a neighborhood bank with "Master Seal Coaters" on the checks and ordered "Master Seal Coaters" business cards from a printer. Then I went door-to-door. I picked out a middle-class neighborhood. The first house I came to had a long drive-way, not in bad shape, but in need of seal coat. A smallish man in his sixties, smoking a cigar, answered my knock on the door. "Hi," I said. "I'm Tom Plummer. I'm a Master Seal Coater. I mean, I seal coat driveways. I notice yours needs attention."

"What?" the man said. He was wearing a hearing aid.

I tried again with more volume. "I seal coat drive-ways."

"How much?" he asked.

"Ten cents a square foot," I said. Max at Coal Tar, Inc., had told me to charge twelve cents a foot, but I needed practice. This was a Grand Opening Sale.

"You're on," he said. "When can you start?"

"Today," I said. I could hardly believe my good fortune.

"I got a job," I yelled as I ran into our house. "I got a seal-coating job on my first door. I'm a Master Seal Coater." Louise and I danced in celebration.

"Ed," I yelled. "Get into your oldest clothes. We're going seal coating." No response. "Ed, come on. You're going to make money."

"Yeah, a dollar an hour," I heard him mutter from the TV room.

We loaded the supplies into the Escort and headed off. I was too excited to pay attention to Ed, who was crouched against the door of the car in a stupor. I wanted him to be as happy as I was. He couldn't have cared less, he has told me a thousand times since. He reminds me every time seal coating creeps into a conversation that I broke every child-labor law on the books.

We hosed down the driveway, cranked up the blower—which was powerful enough to blow a dog into the next block—scrubbed, filled, and prepared to seal coat. I dragged the first bucket out of the car and set it in the driveway. Using a mixing board I had brought from home, I began to stir. It was a hot day, and by now I was sweating badly. As I bent over the bucket, my glasses slipped off my nose. I grabbed for them and missed. They sank to the bottom of the tar. Ed showed his first sign of enthusiasm, letting out a muffled guffaw.

I gingerly reached into the bucket and pulled my glasses out. I rinsed them off carefully with a hose, dried them, and put them back on. I gave less careful attention to my arm. Too irritated, in too much of a hurry, I just wiped off the excess goo with my free hand and got back to work. Ed smiled all day. Thirteen years later he drew me a special Father's Day card to commemorate that moment.

After an hour or two, I noticed that the arm I had dipped into the seal coat was burning. Only later did I learn that seal coat accelerates sunburn. By day's end I had $125 for the driveway, third-degree burns on my right arm, and a son who could not quit talking about how funny it was when my glasses fell into the tar. I also had a business. Two neighbors of the first customer had noticed our careful work and signed on for seal coating.

The next day Louise and I drove past a 1971 green and white Chevy three-quarter-ton truck with a sign on it: $500. "I need that truck," I told her.

"You said you didn't need a truck." Her tone was emphatic.

"I lied," I said. "If I buy that truck I can save 80 percent on seal coat in bulk, make one-tenth the trips to the supplier, and spend more time working. Besides," I said,

# HAPPY FATHERS DAY
## MY DAD LOVES ME, HE TEACHES ME HOW TO WORK

"it's only a matter of time until I have a major spill in the Escort, and then it's done for."

I bought the truck, even though, I learned, it had bad brakes and I had no money to fix them. I bought four fifty-five-gallon drums for the coal tar, which Coal Tar, Inc., filled from giant spigots behind the warehouse. They weighed 600 pounds each at capacity. I bought several bags of sand to mix in. And here I faced a problem I had not anticipated: how to mix the sand into the coal tar. If it was hard in a five-gallon pail, I realized, it would be nearly impossible in a fifty-five-gallon drum.

"Use a shovel," Max said. "Climb up on the drums and stir with a shovel. You'll have to use some muscle."

The memory of losing my glasses in a five-gallon pail while stirring was much too vivid.

"Or," he went on, "you can buy a mixer for $2,500—I have one in the back—or a combination sprayer-mixer for $10,000."

Suddenly I knew how he made money. But not from me. I was broke.

Louise's sister, Janie, and her husband, Ken, were in

Minnesota visiting us. I showed the drums to Ken, a general handyman type, and explained the problem.

"That's easy," he said. "You buy an electric motor and mount it shaft-down on the lid of a drum. Then you make a giant hook out of lead pipe that can stir the coal tar and sand in the drum. It's like mixing bread on a larger scale."

I was skeptical at first, but Ken seemed to know what he was talking about. I bought a motor and pipe, and in twenty-four hours I had a mixer.

Then I recruited Charles, son number three, who was ten, to the work crew. His job was to run the blower and spray the water while Ed and I spread coal tar. We became a real operation. My motto: Do each driveway perfectly. For every job, three more customers lined up, because they liked what they saw. Louise drove out to work sites each day with lunch in her father's bucket.

About this time our oldest son, Jon, fourteen, returned from camp. He had missed the whole undertaking until now, and his brothers took pleasure in showing him the filthy truck with drums, tools, buckets, and sand. I cannot recall his exact words, but they had something to do with us being nuts.

"You're going to help," I said. "Put on your oldest, crummiest clothes, because you're going to get dirty. We leave at 5:30 A.M."

Jon was ready to go at break of day. He stood before us in a new white T-shirt, white pants, and white tennis shoes. Charles and Ed looked at each other and grinned.

"You're going to get dirty," I said. "And your clothes won't come clean. Put on something else."

"This is what I'm wearing, and I won't get dirty. I'm not a pig," he said. His jaw was set in a stubbornness I knew well. I decided to let come what inevitably would.

Our job that day was at the very large driveway of a manufacturer named Hassleman. It made a huge semicircle from the street to the front door of the house. Another road—it was about that big—went from the street to the garage at the rear of the house. The surface totaled about 10,000 square feet, and that meant a lot of money at twelve cents a foot.

We had to carry the coal tar in five-gallon buckets from the truck, which was parked on the street, to the areas we were surfacing. To get the coal tar from the drums, we used a barrel cradle to turn them on their sides. Tight lids kept the coal tar inside. I had put a faucet on each drum lid, so that we could just turn the handle and coal tar would come out. I sent Jon to fill a bucket. It was his first errand.

Ed, Charles, and I stopped working to watch. Jon stepped to the drum, held the bucket under the spigot, and turned it on. The tar gushed out, splashing over the side of the bucket, down his shirt and pants, and onto his shoes. He stood there in disbelief, now initiated into the brotherhood of seal coaters.

Over the summer we put down 250,000 square feet of seal coat. We ended the season's work on Labor-Day weekend doing the parking lot of Mr. Hassleman's manu-facturing plant, 30,000 square feet. We worked twelve hours a day for three days, and when we were finished it looked beautiful. That night, while the surface was still wet, a smart aleck on a new BMW motorcycle, looking for a place to do popper wheelies, sped past the barriers we had set up, skidded on the tar, and dumped his machine and himself in his new leathers all over the black stuff. He was still waiting for us in the morning when we came to check the job. Coal tar all over himself and his machine, mad as a banty rooster. I wondered how he would have that motorcycle sandblasted. He spit out demands for compensation. I told him that, although I felt sorry for his mess, he had crossed warning barriers and driven onto private property.

He threatened to sue Mr. Hassleman, who in turn told him he would have him arrested for trespassing. The biker gave up and left with his blackened bike and sticky leathers unreimbursed.

It was a fitting end to the most productive summer of my life. I learned that it was nice to receive cash on the spot for a job when I completed it. At the university I was salaried, so that the teaching and writing I did had no apparent connection with the money I received.

I learned that there is always work. If I lost my job, I could create work. I was, by close of summer, just a step away from establishing my own business, from becoming my own boss, from controlling my own hours, from taking charge of my own life. Instead of being subject to evaluations by colleagues with political agendas, I would be responsible only to customers who decided whether I was good enough for another job another time.

I learned that for the first time Louise thought I was working hard enough to deserve a lunch. I earned a lunch every day that summer, and every day she delivered it, smiling and full of affection. I was her "man."

I learned there were folks in the world who worked hard for a living. Late one day I was standing at the end of a driveway assessing what I had done. A roofer who was working on a neighbor's house came over to talk.

"They delivered my *#@$ shingles to the wrong @$*& house," he said. He was a small man, wiry, muscular, burned and scarred by too many years in the sun, and incapable of speaking without four-letter words.

"Boy, that's bad news," I said. "What are you going to do?"

"Well, I called the #@$* trucker and he's going to pick up the *#@$ shingles and move them to the right #@$& house tomorrow morning."

Even as he spoke, I felt like I was having an out-of-body experience, looking down on myself having a conversation—on no deep topic, but a conversation nonetheless—with a roofer. I was flattered, genuinely flattered, that he would talk to me, that he saw me as one of his kind. Workmen who had come to our house to make repairs could not talk to me that way. They saw the decor of the house, the shelves lined with books, and they kept their mouths shut.

When he left, Charles said, "Dad, do you think he knew you had a Ph.D. from Harvard?"

"No," I said. "I don't think he would have talked to me if he had."

It was a good day.

Soft as the voice of an    an  -  gel

Breath-ing a    les-son  un  -  heard

Hope with a  gen-tle  per - sua  -  sion

Whispers her com-fort-ing word    —

WHISPERING HOPE
BY ALICE HAWTHORNE

# The Prayer Tree

About the time of my fiftieth birthday, I read an article that said fifty is the body's turning point toward failing health. That didn't describe me. I was running five miles a day, thinking about training for a marathon, and weighing in with just 10 percent body fat. I had the leanness of my mother's family, where people live well into their eighties and nineties, not the stockiness of my father's family, where people die in their sixties and seventies. I would live as long as my mother. I was a new Methuselah.

I was deluded. On the morning of December 23, 1991, I stood in front of the bathroom mirror, shaving. As I dragged the razor over my whiskers, I noticed that my reflection seemed more blurred than usual. Was it possible that my 20/500 vision had become worse overnight? I was squinting and closing one eye and then the other to see myself clearly enough to shave. I could scarcely see my sideburns.

When I finished, I went to the bookcase to test my vision on titles. I started with glasses off. I couldn't read a thing, not even close up. I put them on. Everything was double. Two biographies of Carol Burnett, two copies of *Sex, Death, and Fly Fishing,* two *Tales of Two Cities.* I could see properly only by shutting one eye. I picked up the phone, called my opthamologist, Larry Noble, and described my problem to his receptionist.

"Come in at ten this morning," she said.

Then I called my neurologist friend, Al Wirthlin. "Al," I said, "I'm seeing double. What's going on?"

"I don't know," he said. "Are you seeing double vertically or horizontally?"

"Horizontally," I said. "Book titles on the shelf are

doubled side by side. I've already made an appointment with an opthamologist."

"Well, go see him first," he said. "If he doesn't know what's wrong, I should probably examine you. It's nothing to worry about." I didn't believe him. I remembered him saying once that double vision was symptomatic of big trouble. I just couldn't remember what the big trouble was.

Larry, the opthamologist, projected a single dot on the wall in front of me. "How many dots do you see with both eyes open?" he asked.

"Two."

"How many do you see with the right eye closed?"

"One."

"How many do you see with the left eye closed?"

"One."

"When you see two dots, are they side by side, or is one above the other?"

"Side by side."

He faced me with his arms folded. "Let's call your neurologist friend," he said.

I couldn't understand most of the conversation. Larry

filled his sentences with medical terminology except when he said, "Yeah, that's what worries me too."

He put me on the phone with Al. "Listen, Tom," Al said, "I'm going to order an MRI so I can have a look at your brain tonight. It'll rule out some things, and then you and Louise can take off for San Francisco after Christmas like you've planned. This is nothing."

I was not reassured. As we turned into University Hospital that night, I muttered to Louise, "If this is nothing, why am I having a $1,200 brain scan?"

By the time I finished the MRI, Al and his wife, Virginia, had joined Louise. "Sit down," Louise said. "Al has something to tell you." Her voice had the same serious tone as when she had told me that our son had been picked up for shoplifting.

"Tom," Al said, "you have a very large, benign pituitary tumor. It's in the middle of your head on the underside of your brain." He made a circle with his thumb and forefinger to suggest its size. "You'll have to have surgery."

Over the next twenty-four hours, I learned from a second opthamologist that the double vision could be permanent, and from an endocrinologist, a neurosurgeon, and Al that the surgery involved making an incision between my gum and upper lip, pulling my face up and back like a rubber mask, inserting a camera and surgical tools alongside the nasal passage, and reaming the tumor out like a cantaloupe. They would be working around the carotid arteries, the optic nerves, and the section of the brain governing motor control. This surgery, they told me, was new, developed in the last few years. Previously surgeons cut off the top of the head, dehydrated the brain to a fraction of its original size, and then worked underneath it on the pituitary. Our bishop, who was a doctor, called it "a benign tumor in a malignant place."

In the next days of testing, I considered the entire procedure to be in the hands of the doctors. They were experienced, reassuring, and confident. I was not prepared, then, for the thought that entered my mind three or four days after the diagnosis. It was early morning, still dark. I was dozing-thinking-dreaming about surgery. A scripture came into my mind: "This kind cometh not out but by fasting and by prayer."

I had no idea where the passage came from, although I suspected the New Testament. I found it in the story of a man who brought his son to Jesus to be healed. The son was possessed by a dumb spirit. When the boy saw Jesus, "the spirit tare him; and he fell on the ground, and wallowed foaming." Jesus offered to help the distraught father, saying, "If thou canst believe, all things are possible to him that believeth."

The father knew his faith was incomplete and said to Jesus, "Lord, I believe; help thou mine unbelief."

Jesus then took the son by the hand and "lifted him up; and he arose" (Mark 9:17-29). The disciples had already tried to heal the boy and asked Jesus why they couldn't. Jesus answered, "This kind can come forth by nothing, but by prayer and fasting" (Mark 9:29). That was the line that had come to me.

As I read the story, I realized that the key to my cure was both physical and spiritual. It depended as much on my fasting and prayer as it did on the skill of the doctors. I was both physically and spiritually sick, and the cure, likewise, must be both physical and spiritual. At that moment, the idea seemed more like a threat than a help. The responsibility had shifted from the doctors to me. Did

I have enough faith to make this happen? How would I bring it about?

I wondered who might give me a blessing, who understood the healing process as Jesus understood it. His words to the disciples weighed heavy: their faith was insufficient. I needed a healer with faith.

I recalled a conversation I'd had one night with my neighbor Bob Bennion. We were walking somewhere along the trail in Rock Canyon with our wives. We got onto the subject of blessings and healing. Bob told about the Navajo way: "They might give the sick person a drink or touch him with feathers," he said, "but while they are doing that they keep talking about the Savior—as they understand Him—coming. They only invite Him when they need Him, because His power is so great He can be dangerous. They sing and then feel Him coming."

He paused while we negotiated some rocks on the trail. "Then they say very specific things about the healing process," he continued. "They don't just say 'get better' or 'heal' or 'we ask God to heal you.' They say 'Happily my fever is leaving,' or 'Happily my blood is flowing better,' or 'Happily the pain in my side is going away.' They focus on the particular organism that is sick and use faith to bring it back into the harmony that the Creator wants."

I wanted the kind of blessing Bob had described, focused right on the tumor. I called him on New Year's Day and asked him to fast and pray about giving me a blessing. I did not remind him of our earlier conversation in Rock Canyon, because I did not want to interfere with his impressions. We agreed to have the blessing the night before surgery, which was scheduled for January 9.

A day or two later Louise and I were talking in our living room. "Tom," she said, "I want you to get well. But to plead with God to heal you when millions of other people are dying of brain tumors and cancer and diabetes—it just doesn't seem fair. I can't do it." Her voice cracked. We sat there for some time, saying nothing. When she finally stood up to leave the room she said, "I know what I'll do."

Passing her study on my way to the bedroom, I noticed she was cutting a yellow legal pad into dozens of slips of paper, each about 1/4 inch wide and 8 inches long. Then I knew. We had gone to Japan for our twenty-fifth wedding anniversary. At one of the Buddhist temples, a woman was selling prayers on slips of paper. Each was addressed to Buddha to protect the petitioner from evil. The patron would read the message and then tie it on a nearby tree. Little white papers, resembling blossoms in the bright morning sun, covered the tree.

The next morning I walked into the living room to find our ficus tree covered with yellow slips of paper, each tied in an overhand knot. The tree seemed to be full of yellow ribbons. In the Japanese tradition, Louise had written something on each slip. I carefully untied them and read:

Tom buys a snazzy 4 x 5 camera

Tom and Louise in New York City in spring of 1992

Tom's patch comes off and double vision is gone, January 1992

Tom and Louise go to Hawaii for Christmas, 2005

Tom catches big fish with worm in Deep Lake in 1992

Tom drives with Louise in open convertible to Mirror Lake and back every summer starting 1992

Tom loses 12 pounds in 1992

Tom can beat up any of his sons in 1992

Tom goes for walks with Louise well into the 2020s

Tom and Louise buy Mayflower condo in 1995

Tom buys new truck in 1997

Tom ordains Charles an elder in 1993

Tom and Louise spend a year in Holland in 1998

Tom writes a book of essays in 1994, 1998, 2005, 2010, etc.

Tom buys a cashmere overcoat in 1993

Tom has 20/25 vision after operation in January 1992

Tom and Louise go to the symphony in February 1992

Tom and Louise go to Italy in 1996—Rapallo

Tom ordains Sam an elder in 1998

Tom and Louise drink orange spice tea from china cups in 1992

Tom catches large rainbow trout in Provo River with fly rod—spring 1994

As I sat on the floor by the tree, with the pile of slips in front of me, I saw sketches of my future extending well into the 2020s. I read and reread them, and then I tied all the slips on the tree again. Every day I would open a few at random just to refresh my memory. I left the tree decorated that way for months. When the papers began to tear, I copied their contents onto a sheet of paper and put them in a zip-lock bag that I kept in my desk.

On the night before surgery, Bob and Francine Bennion, Phil and Pat Daniels (our neighbors), Louise, and our four sons gathered in our living room. We knelt together. Louise gave an invocation so heartfelt and loving that I opened my eyes to watch her. Then Bob, with Phil and our sons, proceeded with the blessing. Bob instructed my body to stop recruiting the blood supply for the tumor, and to shut down the vessels that were transporting the blood to it. When the blessing ended, I was no longer afraid.

Sometime later Bob told me that he had been outside in the garden after I asked for the blessing. As he worked, the idea of the Navajo prayers returned to him. "I realized that Heavenly Father and the Savior knew how to instruct Tom to cut off the blood that was feeding the tumor," he said.

I know that someday I will die, that someday my body and spirit will not respond. I know that my vision of a life on earth, dancing with Louise, wrestling with my sons, riding through autumn leaves in a convertible, will end. I don't know when. I don't know why several of my friends have died and I have not. I don't know why they suffered and I have not yet suffered.

So what good is faith if it can't guarantee life? Others have not been healed by their faith. Others, as Louise so succinctly said, are dying of cancer, diabetes, or heart disease. Others die in accidents or in war. For me, faith brings peace, spiritual healing, relief from fear and anxiety. It connects me with God. It empowers me to live a fuller and more creative life and gives me a vision of eternal life.

Come a-way with me, Lu - cile        In   my

mer - ry  Olds-mo - bile     Down the  road  of

life we'll   fly,      Au-to-mo-bub-bling, you and I.

IN MY MERRY OLDSMOBILE
BY VINCENT BRYAN AND GUS EDWARDS

# Once in Your Life Own a Convertible

While I was in the hospital recovering from surgery, our friends Gene and Dorothy Bramhall dropped off *Life's Little Instruction Book* for my amusement. Louise sat at the side of my bed reading the 500 pithy bits of advice for biophiles. "77. Don't take health for granted." Done. "79. Don't mess with drugs, and don't associate with those who do." No problem. "116. Consider writing a living will." Not funny. "211. Take your dog to obedience school. You'll both learn a lot." Too late. "242. Be cautious about lending money to friends. You might lose both." Broke. "406. Read hospital bills carefully. It's reported that 89 percent contain errors—in favor of the hospital."

I was dozing off when Louise said, "Hey. Here's one I love." I jolted awake. "32. Once in your life own a convertible."

Through the haze I could see her on her feet. She was clasping her hands, fingers interlocking, the way she does when she's really excited. The way she does when, as she puts it, she has found "truth (=beauty)."

"We need a Miata," she said.

For noninitiates, the Miata is a little roadster manufactured by Mazda. It is the best-looking roadster since the squarish MGs with the pentagonal grill of the 1950s, only the Miata really runs. "We're going to get a Miata. Yes." She was dancing around the room.

I muttered something about three sons still at home and a convertible being an impractical idea. "Yes," she was saying, "a Miata. We'll get a Miata."

I faded back into the haze. A gnawing told me this would not go away.

During the next few months of recovery, I kept my distance from the Miata idea. The family was too large. We had two vehicles, a passenger car and a pickup truck that I used for fishing. We needed the car for the family, the truck for hauling things around in—mostly my fishing gear.

"Miatas make great trucks," Louise said one day as I chewed my breakfast of Golden Grains. She was taking a new tack.

"What are you talking about?"

"Miatas make great trucks. You put the top down and you can haul a lot of lumber. It just sticks out of the top. A Miata will do anything your truck will do, and it's a convertible. You could go fishing in a Miata. They're so beautiful. Let's just go look at them today."

I have never been able to say no to an invitation to go out with Louise. Not that shopping trips are always successful. Sometimes we come home depressed. We see things we can't afford—like luxury homes and Miatas—and then we go nuts thinking about how we can get them anyway. Are there any deposits for us in a Swiss bank from deceased people we never knew?

But sometimes we find wonderful deals. When we needed a dining-room table, we went to furniture stores all over Minneapolis. The cheap ones were ugly—unacceptable to an aesthete—and the expensive ones were off the charts. Finally we wandered into Gabbert's odds-and-ends room. I went to the bathroom while Louise looked around. I came out to find her draped over a Henredon Queen-Anne table, in perfect condition except that the support block on one leg underneath the table was broken. A screw would fix it. The price: $99. The delivery man offered us $300 cash on the spot when he brought it.

Did the Mazda dealer have an odds-and-ends room? "Well, they start at $15,000," the salesman was saying. He was about twenty years old. Green as grass, as my mother would say. "But we don't have any of those in stock. Our 'A' models start at $17,000, our 'B' models at blah blah blah." I stood there in shock and utter dismay. Actually, they cost less than most sedans and a lot less than the pickup trucks and four-wheel-drive vehicles and vans that jam the roads in Utah County. But those people have an excuse for buying mega-cars. They have lots of kids and tons of groceries to haul. What's my excuse for the Miata? It's fun? You aren't supposed to have a car for fun.

Louise was walking around a black, special-edition model with tan leather seats. She ran her fingers lovingly over it. "It's so beautiful," she said. "We could go for long rides with the top down. I'd go fishing in it with you."

"And hold my gear in your lap?" I slipped into sarcasm.

"Yes, I'd do that." Her reply was quick and sure. "And this is April. A perfect time to be getting a Miata."

I could feel myself starting to sweat. "Come on, we have to think about this. We can't afford that black one," I said. Even as I let the words slip out, I realized I had made a concession. I had blinked, as a friend in real estate says. We can't afford the black one, but I haven't said no to the red ones. This did not elude her.

A few weeks passed, and I was accepted for a workshop for university faculty in Berlin for June and July. I felt slightly guilty about leaving, but after five months of confinement recovering from surgery, I decided to go. Soon after I had accepted, as I was dozing off for the night, Louise said, "It'll replace sex."

"Huh?" I tried to piece together what might have led to this comment.

"It'll replace sex while you're in Germany," she said. "The Miata. It's better than sex." I struggled to assemble my faculties. "I won't use that dumb pickup truck while you're gone. It's ugly. You haven't been fishing for months. I want a convertible to drive around while you're gone. We can trade in the truck on it."

The Miata was delivered the day before I left for Berlin. "Oh, goody," Louise repeated over and over. "Now I won't be so lonely."

I haven't figured out the relationship between sex and the Miata, and I haven't figured out how it overcame her loneliness in my absence. I don't want to know. But I have learned that the Miata really is a fine truck. I have hauled lumber in it, eight-foot boards protruding out of the open top. I have transported trees, mute passengers beside me waving their branches in the breeze. With Louise I have taken it up the Provo River fishing a few times, she holding my rod case, which won't fit into the trunk. It draws stares from the pickup-truck crowd.

But in the end, the Miata is therapy for the weary psyche. On warm summer evenings, on cool spring and fall mornings, driving along a canyon stream, driving through neighborhoods wrapped in blankets with the breeze in our hair, I say to Louise, "We must always have a convertible." She slips her hand onto my knee. Once in your life own a convertible.

No- bod- y knows the trou-ble I've seen,

Glo - ry   Hal - le   -   lu - jah!

NOBODY KNOWS THE TROUBLE I'VE SEEN
TRADITIONAL

# OD'd on Shrimp

One night after a shrimp dinner at the Ling Ling Panda, Louise broke into hives. We were at a university gala dance when, in the middle of a slow number, I noticed she was scratching her wrist. We would dance a few steps, then she'd free her right hand and scratch her left wrist behind my head. Then she would take her left hand from my neck and scratch her right wrist.

"I've got hives," she said. "They're breaking out on my hands and arms. Look." Sure enough, large red welts were forming.

"Do you want to leave?" I asked.

"No, let's dance a few more and see how it goes," she said.

I didn't argue. We put cheeks together and danced on. After two or three numbers she said, "We'd better go. I have a serious problem."

By the time we reached home, large welts had formed all over her body. It was nearly 11:00 P.M., and pharmacies were closed. I called the doctor's emergency number. "This isn't a big problem," he assured me. "Go down to Smith's (the twenty-four-hour grocery store) and get a bottle of Benadryl. Have her drink a quarter cup. It'll stop the hives and she'll sleep like a baby." Both were true. The hives subsided, and she slept until noon.

We were not sure what had caused the hives. We suspected the shrimp, possibly the MSG in the shrimp, but quite possibly something unrelated. After that, Louise ate shrimp periodically—especially at Chinese restaurants. For a long time there were no more allergic reactions. Then, maybe one time in five, she would break out. We kept Benadryl around, and when a hive or two emerged, she'd take the usual quarter cup and pass out for the night. "I like my shrimp with a Benadryl chaser," she would say to friends.

One night we went to China Lily's with our good friends Al and Ginny Wirthlin. They like to order a lot of different foods and share dishes. I enjoy that too, but Louise is very clear about what she wants. She wants what she orders, and she doesn't want to share. "If I had wanted your Szechuan beef, I'd have ordered it for myself," she told Al. "I just want shrimp, and I want all of it." So Al, Ginny, and I ordered food to share, and Louise ordered shrimp for herself.

Maybe the cook was drunk that night. Her plate was piled high—at least two dozen shrimp. Louise squealed and clasped her hands. "Oh, goody. I'm going to eat every last one." While the rest of us ate communally, Louise gorged on the shrimp. "Boy, was that good," she said as she finished the last piece. "I'm glad I didn't have to share."

For a short while there were no aftereffects. We sat in the restaurant and talked; then the Wirthlins took us home. As their car pulled away, Louise grabbed my arm and said, "My tongue is swelling up." She guzzled

Benadryl from the bottle, which didn't improve the condition. Her breathing was becoming labored.

"Come on," I said, "let's get you to the emergency room. Tell the doctor you OD'd on shrimp."

When we arrived at the hospital, her breathing was a bit better. "Let's just sit here in the parking lot for a few minutes," she said. "I think it's going away." After a half hour she said, "I think we can go now."

As we lay snuggling in bed that night, she said, "You think I'm stupid, don't you?"

"No," I said. "You just OD'd." Then I laughed.

The next day she called the Wirthlins to tell them what had happened. "It's God's punishment," Al said. "You wouldn't share."

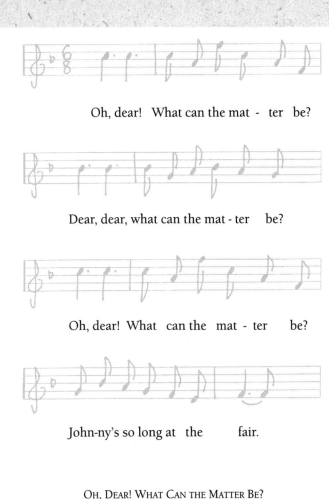

Oh, dear!   What can the mat - ter be?

Dear, dear, what can the mat - ter    be?

Oh, dear!  What   can the   mat - ter     be?

John-ny's so long at   the        fair.

**OH, DEAR! WHAT CAN THE MATTER BE?**
TRADITIONAL

# New York, New York

Recently Louise, Sam, and I went to New York. Louise and I had a lean budget, and lean budgets are incompatible with New York City. Sam had saved money from summer work, so he was loaded. It was an awkward situation: two broke parents with a wealthy teenager.

Louise and I figured we had enough for our favorite treats: the Metropolitan Museum, the Guggenheim, the Frick, and a ride on the Staten Island ferry past the Statue of Liberty. But because I was guardian of the budget, I felt responsible to defend it. I cautioned Louise and Sam over and over, "Don't spend extra money. We just don't have it this time."

"I won't," Louise said. "You just worry about yourself."

We checked into our cheapo hotel, the Pickwick Arms, with its postage-stamp-size room and folding cot for Sam. With his bed down, we could just barely get to the bathroom. No matter. We were in New York. We changed clothes and went out into streets filled with noxious air and honking cabs. We had a light supper, more expensive than I would have liked, at the Rockefeller Center and headed down Fifth Avenue. We stopped at a linen store, where Louise bought place mats and napkins. Had she heard my precautions? My stomach jumped as I paid for them, but I kept my composure.

We crossed over and started up the other side of the street. Directly across from the linen store was one of those little New York electronic shops, windows crammed with cameras, stereos, and CD players. Huge yellow and black banners hung around the windows declaring, "GOING OUT OF BUSINESS SALE." Sam was looking for an adapter plug and went inside.

A group of cameras near the front of the display had unbelievably low prices, so low that I stopped to make calculations.

"Are those good prices?" Louise asked.

"Yeah," I said, "but there's nothing here that I really want. I was just curious to see if they had a point-and-shoot with a 35 to 135 mm zoom lens. I think I'll ask." And I walked inside. I walked inside a sleazy little electronics store in Manhattan with "GOING OUT OF BUSINESS" banners hung all over the front windows. Our friend Ann Cannon has since told Louise that someone did a study on those stores. Most of them claim they are going out of business but never do.

A man with shifty eyes, black mustache, greasy hair, and a thick accent asked me what I was looking for.

"Oh, I was just wondering if you had a point-and-shoot camera with something like a 35 to 135 mm zoom lens on it," I said. I tried to act casual.

He pulled a box imprinted with "Pentax IQZoom 140" off the shelf and opened it. It had an AF/Infinity landscape shutter, an LCD panel, a mode button, red-eye reduction flash button, built-in flash, self-timer, and a zoom from 38 to 140.

"How much is it?" I asked.

"Three hundred and twenty-nine dollars," he said.

I was standing there fondling the camera when Louise came in to see what was keeping me. She examined it, looked through the viewfinder, and tried out the zoom. "How much is it?" she asked.

"It's $329," I said.

"Buy the camera," I heard her say, and she walked back outside. "Buy the camera."

"Will you take $300?" I asked.

"I never bargain," he said.

"Will you take American Express?"

"Yes," he said, "but then you have to give me $100 in cash."

I knew he said this because American Express charges merchants more for using its services than other credit cards.

"I don't have $100 with me," I said. "I've only got $60, and I'm not giving that to you." I had left the rest of the cash in the hotel so I wouldn't make rash decisions.

Before the whole thing was over he had sold me the camera, a battery for $40, and a carrying case for $30. My total bill, including tax, was about $425.

I strolled out of the store with the new camera in the carrying case slung over my shoulder.

"What took you so long?" Louise asked. Spying the camera case she said in a loud voice, "Did you buy that camera?"

I looked around to see if anyone was watching. "Yes," I said, "you told me to."

"I said, 'Don't buy the camera. *Don't*,'" her tongue popped the "d" and spit out the "t."

I felt my whole head flush.

"How much did you pay?"

"About $425," I said. I was hot with embarrassment.

"My gosh, I could have gotten the living-room chair slipcovered for less than that," she said.

My insanity washed over me. I had told Louise and Sam that the New York trip must cost no more than $500, and on the first afternoon I spent $425 on a camera that I had never intended to buy. I looked at the American Express receipt. "No Refunds" was stamped on it in big black letters. What was I thinking? What on earth could I have had in mind? How could I have suspended my own rules inside that sleazy little store that was not going out of business at all? How could I have been such a sucker?

Almost in beat with the questions banging in my head, Louise said (because she was not going to be finished with me for some time), "What you need to be asking yourself, Tom, is why you would buy the camera even if I *had* told you to. You are the one who's worried about money."

"I've never seen him do something like that before," Sam said. "He just pulled out his card and bought it."

I sank deep inside myself. Walking up the sidewalk in a fog, I heard Louise and Sam snickering behind me. I turned around. They were about ten feet back, grinning widely. "Sam feels sorry for you," Louise said. "You look pathetic." They put their arms around me. I didn't deserve a hug. I had been stupid beyond belief. The words "psychotic break" kept coming to mind. I'd had a psychotic break. I'd like to think I had a psychotic break. Carl Jung would say more accurately that an unpredictable and compulsive part of my personality had just popped out, a little shadow that I had been repressing. It was not a psychotic break at all. It was perfectly consistent with my dark side.

"We forgive you," she said. "I'm sure it will be a fine camera. But I'm going to tell everyone I know."

When we got home, and friends asked about our trip, Louise would smile and say, "You tell them all about New York, Tom. I'll fill in the details."

Buf - fa- lo gals won't you come out to-night and

dance by the light of the   moon?

BUFFALO GALS
TRADITIONAL

# Eating Chocolates and Dancing in the Kitchen

A few years ago, just before Christmas, I ran into my friend Jim Faulconer at a checkout counter in the BYU Bookstore. Given my tension about Christmas shopping, I thought Jim was disgustingly cheerful.

"Merry Christmas," he said.

"Drop dead," I snapped.

We both had our arms full of Christmas presents—

books, art supplies, and aftershave. I had a headache. I was already thinking about my next stop at See's Candy in the Orem Mall, where, I imagined, hordes of people would be lined up behind one person who was buying ten boxes of chocolate, each one handpicked and therefore taking about ten minutes to fill. I anticipated being in line for at least an hour. My only incentive for going there at all was to get the free piece of chocolate See's gives to each customer.

I'm not particularly proud of my attitude in that moment. Each year I try to have a merry Christmas, and each year I get a little better at it. Each year Louise and I go to a few more Christmas performances—a Messiah sing-along, a symphony Christmas concert, a choral production, a recital, to keep ourselves focused on what Christmas is about.

Sometimes I wonder if being "merry" at Christmas is a little old-fashioned—like a Currier and Ives painting with horse-drawn sleighs and winter landscapes. Maybe being "merry" is out-of-date—like the word itself.

It seems outmoded for my harried life, as does the verse in Proverbs that says: "A merry heart doeth good

like a medicine: but a broken spirit drieth the bones"
(17:22). Sometimes I'm more inclined to drying my bones.
Sometimes my broken spirit, no matter how unjustified in
comparison with the suffering of others, gets in the way
of my having a merry heart.

I was probably in such a state of mind not long ago,
quietly eating my homemade, no-fat pasta with seafood—
which older men eat to control weight and cholesterol—
when Louise asked, "How do you want to spend the last
quarter of your life?" I stopped eating to register what she
had just said. It seemed unsavory. I don't want to talk
about death when I'm eating. But Louise likes to stir
things up. She times her most disturbing comments to
catch me when I'm vulnerable.

The assumptions of her question were clear enough: I
was no longer middle-aged, I was three-quarter-aged; I was
in a rut; I could die in the rut. I wasn't living my life to the
fullest.

It recalled a moment I'd had with my father more than
thirty years before. He was dying of cancer. I was standing by his bed at LDS Hospital. He asked how my studies
were going. I said I would be glad when the week was

over, because I had an exam on Friday that was driving me nuts.

He lay quietly for a few moments staring at the ceiling, his hands folded over his chest. Then he said, "Don't wish your life away."

Cancer had schooled him. I looked at him lying there, his stocky frame bony and wasted, his breathing labored, made possible only with an oxygen mask. Wouldn't he throw this day away? How about tomorrow? He would never teach again. Never campaign for a library again. Never give another talk. All his passion for living could lead nowhere. What was worth living for? His message reverberated in my head: Even bad days are good days. Don't wish your life away. It's a gift. It's the only life you'll have. I stood there young and stupid. I would never die. My days were endless. I could skip unpleasant days.

Louise's question persisted in my mind. I was approaching the age my father had been when he had died. What was I going to do with the rest of my life? I turned to a group of senior men in my church. "I want to know what you think is worth spending your time on," I said. "Men have a life expectancy of about seventy-five.

Some of you are living on borrowed time." There was uneasy laughter. "Now that you know your time is short, tell me what is really important to you."

Lehi Hintze, a retired geologist, spoke first. "I want to spend my time leaving something that will be permanent, have some lasting value to people. I don't want to spend my life doing something that doesn't make a difference."

"What do you do when you get up on Saturday that will make such a difference?" I asked. My tone was tinged with irony, because I can't think of much that I do that makes a real difference.

"I make maps," he said. "Some of them are for professionals; some of them are for anyone who is interested in the same things I am."

He had recently handed out to all the neighbors four-color maps showing geological features of Utah County. They were so detailed that we could see where our own houses sat in relation to earthquake faults. "Did you make the earthquake maps you handed out recently?" I asked.

"Yes," he said.

An obstetrician raised his hand. He had delivered thousands of babies, probably half the youth of the neighborhood where we were living. "I don't have time to do what I really think is important," he said. "I have an eighty-plus-hour work week. Sometimes I have worked a full forty hours by Tuesday, and the week is just getting under way."

Someone asked if he didn't find delivering babies important and satisfying. What could be more wonderful than bringing new life into the world?

"I used to find it valuable and worthwhile," he said, "but now every delivery is just a potential lawsuit." His voice cracked. "I long to do humanitarian service where I can find spiritual satisfaction."

Jack Smith, a retired U.S. Marine officer with bumper stickers declaring, "Proud to be a United States Marine," was in his late seventies. He spoke with a loud, gruff voice. "Things, material things, don't matter to me anymore," he said. "On Saturdays, I like to have my grandkids come and mow the lawn. I teach them how to use the lawn mower, and I like to give them a lot of money for it. I like to give my money to my grandkids. And I like to teach them things. One of my grandsons couldn't throw a baseball. He'd throw like this." He raised his right hand in front of his shoulder and flipped his wrist forward. "Geez," he said, "I just went ballistic when I saw that. I couldn't stand watching him throw that way. He looked like a sissy. So after he cut the lawn, I'd go out and practice throwing the baseball with him. Finally I got him so he could throw the ball, and he's been on baseball teams ever since. That's what I think is important."

Since that discussion, the geologist has continued to make maps, the doctor has gone on a church mission, and Jack Smith, the Marine, has died of a heart attack.

Louise and I have made our own lists of what seems important to us. Here's mine:

> I want to take rides with Louise in a convertible in the evenings;
>
> I want to go back to the art galleries in Florence, to the Louvre in Paris, to Breukelan in Holland;
>
> I want to live in New York City for a year or two with Louise;
>
> I want to learn to play the piano better;
>
> I want to become a better fly fisherman and to tie better fishing flies;
>
> I want to spend more time with my sons;

I want to baby-sit my grandchildren and take Anne
 Louise and Rian and Harrison Xavier to the zoo;

I want to learn to take better photographs;

I want to continue taking walks in the early morning
 as the light is breaking over the mountains;

Whenever I can, I want to listen to the Tabernacle
 Choir sing on Sunday mornings;

I want to hear Mozart's *Requiem* and *The Magic Flute*
 performed live at least a dozen more times.

Here's a list of what Louise finds important to spend
time on:

My work—writing and teaching—is important, because
 it's an expression of who I am. I get to use my personality in writing and teaching;

Relationships are important—although I don't have
 time for too many relationships except for my family. Almost everything else that's important comes
 under that—taking rides with Tom, trying to listen
 to our son Sam at night, who's sprawled on the
 bed;

I need to have change, to move around. Traveling and

moving around is exciting. I want to stir things up a bit;

I'd like to learn how to play "The Lark and the Clear Air" on the flute;

I want to paint more stars on a wall somewhere;

I don't want to do things out of duty, only out of passion—let the duty lovers do things out of duty;

I always want to give money to people on the street—it's such a hard way to make a living. We're all conning somebody anyway;

I want to dress up in a costume once in a while;

I will continue to sing to canned music in the grocery store;

I want to concentrate on my body and appreciate what it still *can* do—not what it *can't* do—and how beautiful it is;

It's important to set my own rules and not to live by someone else's. It kills the spirit to follow other people's rules;

I want to love Tom—even when it's hard, I will find ways of loving Tom. It's always rewarding to do so. Everyone's a jackass once in a while.

We revise these lists from time to time, often through dream stories. We create dream stories of things that are important to us. It's a spontaneous ritual that we practice several times a week. It works like this: We are commuting from Salt Lake to Provo, or going for a ride or walk, or sitting in bed, and one of us will say, "Tell me a story." This means, "Tell me a story about our future. I need a shot of optimism, a vision of good things to come." The other one then takes a few deep breaths and begins something like this:

In the summer of 1997, Louise goes to New York City and stays at the Olcott Hotel on the Upper West Side, where she spends two weeks finishing her next book and working with her agent and publisher. She spends her free time going to the Frick Museum, where she sits in a favorite spot by the reflecting pool, attending the Sunday concerts, and strolling along Columbus Avenue. She can walk everywhere now, because her ankle is healed.

Tom flies to Berlin, where he digs out the material he needs to finish an article on *The Blue Angel.* In two weeks he has the rest of the article shaped and ready to write. He now goes to Amsterdam, where he meets Louise, who has flown in from New York. They spend a few days with their good friends the Bracys, and then go to Breukelan, where Louise spent the war years as a child. They stay at their favorite inn, the Slangevecht, and eat lunch and supper on the veranda overlooking the Vecht River and the Crow's Nest across the river (the quaint little house where her parents were married).

They sit at dinner and watch luxury yachts sail up and down the river and men sit along the banks and fish with long, European poles.

In the morning they go to a butcher shop to buy cold cuts for breakfast and lunch, to a cheese shop to buy Dutch Edam and Gouda, and to a candy shop to buy a few pieces of Dutch chocolate to eat during the day.

They walk around Breukelan and look at real-estate pictures in agents' windows and dream about buying a little Dutch cottage on a canal where they could go to write and dream in the summer.

Thus engaged, they sing a little song:

Oh, it's H-A-P-P-Y we are

And F-R- double E, EEEE.

And it's G-L-O-R-Y to know

That we're M-A-R-R-I-E-D.

Then we laugh, because even if the story doesn't come true, even if it's absurd, we've amused ourselves with a story and a song, and what can be more important than that? Didn't the Preacher say in Ecclesiastes, "Live joyfully with the wife whom thou lovest"?

A few years ago at Christmas we invented the Alzheimer's Pop Quiz, which has become our favorite game of attack. We wanted to buy some poinsettias from the local nursery, but neither of us could remember the word *poinsettia*. We kept saying things like "those Christmas plants with the red and green leaves," and "the plant that begins with a 'p' or 'r' or 'h.'"

Finally we decided to set out for the nursery hoping that we would remember the word before we got there. As we drove along, we tried various prompts and phonetic gimmicks, but to no avail. When we arrived, we still couldn't remember the name.

"I'm not going in until I can remember," Louise said. "You go ahead." But I was obsessed with the problem too, so we drove around some more. Finally we came to a

Sprouse-Reitz store that was going out of business. Only a teenage clerk was inside.

"Maybe we can find something in there with a picture and name on it," I said. I could see boxes decorated with flora that appeared to be poinsettias. Louise walked straight to the teenage clerk, grabbed him by the sleeve, and dragged him over to the boxes. The flora were indeed poinsettias. "What kind of plant is that?" she demanded.

He was as stupid as we were. "Duh, I don't know," he said. "A rose?"

"Dummy, that's not a rose," Louise said. She smacked him on the shoulder. "Give me a break." We roared out of the store, leaving the clerk baffled and confused.

Finally we gave up and went back to the nursery. Inside were long rows of green and red plants with the name "poinsettia" plastered all over the place. We could have spared ourselves the trouble.

The idea behind the Alzheimer's Pop Quiz as we now play it is to surprise the other person with a question that he or she could normally answer but can't answer on the spot, because he or she simply can't retrieve the information fast enough. The Alzheimer's Pop Quiz preys on the slower memory retrieval of middle-aged adults.

The quiz begins without warning. We're eating dinner or driving in the car or lying in bed. Our brains are out of gear. One of us ambushes the other with a question: What was the name of that hotel we stayed in last time in New York? Who stars in *Three Men and a Baby?* What kind of a bush did we have in the front yard of our last house? Do you remember our Minneapolis phone number?

The one rule is that the person asking the question must know the answer and be able to supply it when the other person becomes desperate and whines that he or she can't rest without the answer.

Once in a while at night, when the lights are out and one of us is dozing off, the other will whisper through the darkness, "What was the name of that green and red Christmas plant?"

There's always a chance the other one's lost it again.

Just hanging out has become a ritual of our lives. Hanging out means finding a little of Saturday and Sunday in every day of the week, asking even on the worst of days, "What will we do today for fun?" It is a drive to the mountains, a ride through pretty neighborhoods, an ice-cream cone in the park, or hot chocolate and a Danish for breakfast while others are moving and shaking the world.

Some people have a gift for hanging out. Others learn it only after a heart attack or cancer reminds them to enjoy life while they have it. Hanging out means loving life and the person you're with. Here's a list of things we do when we hang out:

Play Backgammon

Play the Alzheimer's Pop Quiz

Daydream stories about our future

Talk about night dreams and analyze them

Take long rides and try to get hopelessly lost

Drive around neighborhoods we love

Make up "what if" fantasies ("What if we won the Publisher's Clearing House Sweepstakes?")

Go to real-estate open houses and chant "o-pen, o-pen, o-pen" on the way

Surf the Internet for real estate in places we love (Coronado, Boston, Prince Edward Island) and imagine living there

Post scriptures on the mirror and memorize them
Walk in the city
Sit in the flower gardens east of Temple Square
Watch and critique TV shows
Go to the movies
Go to the symphony, ballet, and theater
Plan trips, even if we don't take them
Take trips
Go shopping, even if we don't buy anything
Psychoanalyze ourselves
Go to See's Candy, buy two pieces of chocolate, and
    get two sample pieces of chocolate free
Compile lists of what to do when we hang out

My ninety-three-year-old mother has invented ways to hang out with herself. She loves football. She called one day five minutes after the BYU game with Wyoming ended. BYU had kicked a field goal in the last second of an overtime to win by three points. "Did you see that game?" she said. Her voice was shrill. "Wasn't that just the most thrilling thing you've ever seen? I just had to call and talk about it." Then she recited her favorite plays, and we talked about the game for half an hour.

Her eyesight is losing a fight with macular degeneration. To see a football game she has to turn sideways to the television set, which even then is blurry for her. She has been widowed for thirty-two years. She has shrunk from her original five feet one inch to about four feet eight inches, and from 100 pounds to 85 pounds fully dressed. The curvature of her back gives her the profile of a question mark. When I take her shopping or to the doctor, people tend to treat her like a pet mouse. "You're so cute," doting nurses are inclined to say. She's not amused.

She works in her garden in the summer. In the winter, she orders recorded books for the blind from the library and goes through several a week. She simply does not let the idea of death or sadness enter her mind. If you ask her how she is, she says, "I'm just fine." She lives a "merry" life. She allows no broken spirit to dry her bones.

When Florida Scott Maxwell was in her eighties, living alone, she danced by herself. She wrote in her diary: "My kitchen linoleum is so black and shiny that I waltz while I wait for the kettle to boil. This pleasure is for the old who live alone. The others must vanish into their expected role."*

Louise and I dance too. We keep a CD player in the kitchen just for dancing. Sometimes we dance after breakfast, sometimes after dinner. We dance on the hardwood floor to Glen Miller's "In the Mood," or to Les Brown and His Band of Renown playing "Sentimental Journey." On fast numbers we jitterbug and do some moves. I put my right hand behind my back and Louise takes it with her left hand. Then we twist underneath, create an arch, and come together side by side, hands still locked, arms interwoven. Then a final spin and we are back into the normal step. Louise won't do that in public. She is about the same height as I am, and she says I am too short for such moves, that we look clumsy, that ungraceful moves should be reserved for the kitchen.

On slow numbers we dance cheek to cheek, the way we did when we were dating. We do a few spins and a dip or two. We anticipate our favorite pieces, the Four Lads singing "Moments to Remember," Nat King Cole singing

---

*The Measure of My Days* (New York: Penguin, 1979), 28.

"Star Dust," and Jimmy Durante singing "As Time Goes By." We mourn just a bit that the Four Lads are no more, that Nat King Cole and Jimmy Durante are dead, and we wonder how we got so old.

Sometimes our kids watch, baffled that old people still have so much energy, so much passion.

"Gross," they say. "That's really gross."

"Just wait," we say. "Just you wait."

Despite what the children say, I think my father would approve of the way we dance in the kitchen. When we are dancing, we can't wish our lives away.

Afterwards we go to See's for dessert—a dark cherry chocolate for Louise, a chocolate truffle for me, and two free samples. Could it be that the forbidden fruit was really truffles?

LOVE'S OLD SWEET SONG,
BY G. CLIFTON BINGHAM AND J. L. MOLLOY